SAINT FRANCIS
AND HIS FRIENDS

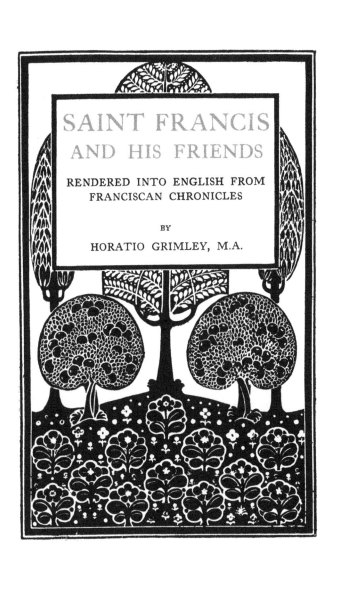

SAINT FRANCIS
AND HIS FRIENDS

RENDERED INTO ENGLISH FROM
FRANCISCAN CHRONICLES

BY

HORATIO GRIMLEY, M.A.

CAMBRIDGE UNIVERSITY PRESS
Cambridge, New York, Melbourne, Madrid, Cape Town,
Singapore, São Paulo, Delhi, Mexico City

Cambridge University Press
The Edinburgh Building, Cambridge CB2 8RU, UK

Published in the United States of America by Cambridge University Press, New York

www.cambridge.org
Information on this title: www.cambridge.org/9781107624764

First published 1908
First paperback edition 2013

A catalogue record for this publication is available from the British Library

ISBN 978-1-107-62476-4 Paperback

TO

ALL FRIENDS OF SAINT FRANCIS

THIS LITTLE BOOK

IS INSCRIBED

WITH BROTHERLY GREETINGS.

No narrow heart is a shrine of the Lord Divine.
He who is Love saith "All, not a part, must be Mine.'
Thou, whose large heart all with tender love embraceth,
Thou in that heart dost shelter Him who all createth.

JACOPONE DA TODI.

CONTENTS.

CONTENTS

INTRODUCTION.

S AINT Francis was led away from earth by
Sister Death in the year 1226. He had been
born in 1182. The forty-four years of the saint's
earthly life included the last seven years of the
reign of Henry II., the whole of the reigns of
Richard Cœur de Lion and of his brother John,
and the first ten years of the reign of Henry III.
During those forty-four years Englishmen were
thus passing through the early days of their
devotion to a saint of their own, Thomas à
Becket, slain by knights in Canterbury Cathedral;
they were excited by the crusading prowess and
adventures of Richard, whom they eagerly
ransomed when imprisoned in an Austrian
castle; they were stirred by the barons' revolt
against John, who had invaded his subjects'
rights, and endangered the national independence
of the English Church. And too there was then
living in England a gentle scholar, Edmund Rich,
destined to be a successor to Thomas à Becket in
the archbishopric of Canterbury, and to seek refuge

as he had done from a king's displeasure in the Abbey of Pontigny, and soon after his death in exile to be acknowledged also as a saint of the Christian Church.

At an earlier date a merchant of Lucca, Bernardo Moriconi, settled at Assisi, the hillside city of Umbria, in which this Introduction is being penned, and carried on there his trade in silk stuffs and cloth. Being tall and massive, he was known as Bernardino, the big Bernard. In Italy such familiar names often perpetuate themselves. Bernard's did. His real surname ceased to be mentioned. He had a son Pietro. This son was always known as Pietro Bernardino. He succeeded to his father's prosperous business. He travelled about with his rich fabrics from castle to castle. He was thus wandering through Provence when he met with her who became his wife. Pica was her name. A son was born to them at Assisi. To this son, Francis, Pica taught the Provençal language. He was ever fond of it. It was the language in which he would often sing as he moved along the Umbrian roads. He was of a gay, troubadour spirit. It was possible for those who acquired wealth as traders in costly products to become in time ennobled. Francis, with his gay temperament and bright prospects, was a welcome companion of the young nobles

of Assisi. With such he took part in a conflict
with the men of Perugia. The result for his
companions and himself was defeat and a year's
imprisonment in Perugia. During the imprisonment he cheered his companions with his songs
and his gay indifference to his lot.

After his return to Assisi he was ill with fever.
The illness was the commencement of a change
in Francis. The change is sometimes called his
conversion. To his natural brightness of disposition there was added a new feeling—a longing,
an aspiration towards things spiritual. There
was added too a desire to minister consolingly to
the poorest of his fellow-creatures, to those most
wasted by disease and misery. After a short
period of uncertainty as to the pathway along
which the spiritual treasures that had been
revealed to him in vision should be sought, and
as to how he might best plan out his life for the
good of others, his decision was made. This was
in 1209, when he was present at Holy Communion
in the chapel of the Portiuncula.

He resolved that henceforth his life should be
conformed to a rule of Gospel simplicity, of
evangelic poverty. He would live only on the
bread of charity. He would clothe himself only
in a coarse gown, girded with a knotted cord.
His feet should always be bare. He would

salute every one he met with a new greeting, "The Lord give thee peace."

His father, grieved at his conduct, became alienated from him. In the home of his youth, only his gentle mother Pica kept her love for him. His friends were perplexed with his changed demeanour. Boys in the streets called after him, and threw at him mud and stones.

Gradually the surprise and astonishment of his friends changed into admiration. His gentle endurance of suffering, his self-chosen toil in helping with his own hands to rebuild ruined sanctuaries, his bright earnestness, drew others to him. Soon there were twelve companions, one an Englishman. The twelve before long increased to a numerous band of followers.

They lived first of all in huts, such as had been assigned as refuges for lepers, who had to live apart from others, until at length the chapel of Saint Mary of the Portiuncula was bestowed upon them. Around this they built little cells, with walls of wattle, rudely plastered, and roofs of straw; the earth being the floor.

Francis thought it well to write down a rule for the guidance of his followers. This rule was confirmed at Rome in 1210 by Pope Innocent III., with whom Francis had a memorable interview. The brotherhood then began its mission-work amongst the people of Umbria and Central Italy. Many others were attracted by Francis's simple but touching appeals to adopt his rule of life.

In Assisi one presented herself to Francis, so that he might listen to her vow of renunciation of the world, and receive her into a life of seclusion and humiliation. She was the daughter of Count Favorino Scifi. Her name was Clara. Soon after, her sister Agnes joined her, and later on her aunt and her mother. A sisterhood was formed, dwelling ultimately in the convent of San Damiano. This is generally spoken of as the Second Order founded by Francis—the Order of the Poor Clares.

Francis, as he carried on his mission-work, preached in market-places, or from the steps of churches. He ventured up to castle courtyards, even on days of festivity, to proclaim the gospel of simplicity and brotherly love. He aroused a widespread enthusiasm. Attracted by the magnetic spell of his presence and by his gentle appeals, more desired to follow him than could be received into the Order, or than could with any prudence leave their homes or desert their wonted avocations. Francis decided to form another Order for such. The members of this

Third Order, which later on included Saint Louis of France and Saint Elizabeth of Hungary, lived in obedience to rules of devotion and duty tending to beneficently transform their daily lives.

Francis planned schemes to carry out which would have taken him to the farthest bounds of Christendom, and even beyond. They cannot be further referred to here.

Francis retired often to lonely scenes. There even the birds and creatures of the woods were susceptible to the charm of his gentle, caressing ways, and entered into loving companionship with him.

The story of his dwelling amid the solitudes of La Verna is reproduced in the following pages from "The Little Flowers of Saint Francis." A brief narrative is given too of his ecstasy there. Then is told how from La Verna, ever since looked upon as a sacred mountain, he came down to Assisi, to die at Saint Mary of the Angels, on the 4th of October, 1226, a day that since Francis's canonization in 1227 by Pope Gregory IX. has been observed with beautiful and impressive devotions as the Festival of Saint Francis.

The Franciscan Order speedily established itself in the principal countries of Europe. It was in September, 1224, that a little company of nine Franciscan friars arrived in England. And thus it happened that during the lifetime of the Saint, Franciscan houses were started in Oxford and Cambridge and in East Anglian towns.

The impress that Saint Francis made upon the mind of Christendom is borne witness to not only by the appealing art of great painters, but also by the various chronicles and legends written by his companions and their successors in the Franciscan brotherhood. In this book selections have been made from : " The Legend of the Three Companions," written in 1246 by Brothers Leo, Angelo, and Rufinus ; "The Little Flowers of Saint Francis," written between 1330 and 1385 by an author unknown; "The Mirror of Perfection," written by Brother Leo in 1228; "The Two Lives of Saint Francis" by Thomas of Celano (1228 and 1246) ; "The Life of Saint Francis" by Saint Bonaventura (1263); and "The Holy Converse of the Blessed Francis with Lady Poverty," attributed to John of Parma.

The chapel of Saint Mary of the Portiuncula, or Saint Mary of the Angels, the first real home of Saint Francis's Order, and the hut too in which he died, are still to be seen beneath the dome of

the great church built in more recent times as a
sacred protecting enclosure. So, also, within the
great convent of La Verna, are still to be seen
the rocks, cells, and caves associated with Saint
Francis's devotions and ecstasies on the sacred
mountain.

HORATIO GRIMLEY.

Assisi.
9 *November*, 1907.

SAINT FRANCIS AND HIS FRIENDS.

I. SAINT FRANCIS IN THE DAYS OF HIS YOUTH.

Francis, born in the city of Assisi, in the Vale of Spoleto, was by his mother first called John; but by his father, in whose absence he had been born, on his return from France, he was afterwards named Francis.

After he had grown up, and had shown himself to be of a refined turn of mind, he practised his father's calling, that is, his business. But he was very unlike his father, since he was more generous, and more given to merriment, fond of jokes and songs, loving to wander through Assisi by day and by night, with those like unto himself as his companions. He was lavish with money, so that what he could get into his hand, or could earn, he would spend in feasting and in other ways. For this reason he was many times scolded by his parents, who used to tell him that he spent so much on himself and others that he did not seem to be a son of theirs, but of some great prince. Since, however, his parents were rich, and had very tender love for him, they bore with him, not caring to vex him in such matters.

His mother, when she heard the neighbours talk about his extravagance, would reply: " What is that that you think of my son? He shall yet be, by grace, the son of God."

Francis was, however, by disposition courteous both in manners and in speech ; according to the intent of his heart speaking to no one a hurtful or disgraceful word. Indeed, even when he was merry and lighthearted, he purposely scarcely answered those who talked to him of shameful things. From this the report of him through well-nigh the whole district was so carried about that by many who knew him it was said that he would in the future be something great.

By which grades of natural goodness he advanced towards such grace that he would thus address himself : " Inasmuch as thou art generous and courteous amongst those from whom thou receivest nothing but some slight and fleeting favour, it is right, since that God is most generous in His rewards, that thou shouldst be courteous and liberal to the poor." Whence from that time did he regard the poor with kindliness, distributing alms to them with eagerness.

When he was one day in the stores where he sold cloth, and was anxious as to the business of the kind there carried on, a poor man came to him, asking alms for the love of God. And when, held back at the moment by the desire for riches and by the thought of selling his wares, he refused alms to the poor man, he forthwith chode himself for his great churlishness, and coming under the influence of divine grace, he said : " If this poor man had demanded from thee something for a great Count, or a Baron, thou wouldst certainly have bestowed on him what he asked for. By how much more then oughtest thou to have given him alms for the sake of the King of Kings and the Lord of all?" For which reason he decided in his heart that henceforth he assuredly would not refuse anything asked for for the sake of so great a Lord.

* * *

At a time when war was going on between Perugia and Assisi, Francis was taken captive with a number of his fellow-citizens, and kept in prison in Perugia. As he was noble in his manners, he was placed as prisoner among the knights. When, however, on a certain day his fellow-prisoners were oppressed with sadness, he, who naturally was merry and lighthearted, did not seem to be sad, but in a way inclined to be sportive; for which reason one of his companions found fault with him, as though he thought him not in his right mind, since forsooth he was glad of heart when shut up in prison. To this one Francis spoke out plainly: "What art thou thinking of me? I shall yet be thought well of by the whole world."

And when one of the knights with him had wrought some harm to a fellow-prisoner, and for this was shunned by the others, who wished to keep themselves apart from him, Francis was the only one not to keep away from him, and encouraged others to do as he did.

At the end of a year there was a restoration of peace, and Francis and his fellow-prisoners returned free to Assisi.

* * *

After a few years a certain nobleman of the city of Assisi, prepared as for war, and essayed to go unto Apulia, seeking to add to his wealth or to gain renown. Hearing of this, Francis had a longing to go with him, and desiring that by a certain count, named Gentile, he might be made a knight, he made lavish preparations for the enterprise.

IN THE DAYS OF HIS YOUTH

One night, when he had given himself up to thinking out how to carry out his desire, and was feverishly longing to start on the adventure, he was visited by the Lord, who as though he were one yearning for glory, allured him onwards and exalted him by the vision to the utmost height of glory.

For, when he was sleeping that night, there appeared unto him one calling him by name, and leading him into a spacious and pleasant palace, full of knightly armour, forsooth dazzling shields and other apparel hanging on the wall, as though in readiness for knights to array themselves therewith. When he, in greatness of joy, looked around in silent wonder as to what it all meant, he asked whose might be the arms shining with such splendour, and the palace so delightful. And answer was made to him that all those things and the palace were for himself and his knights.

And then arising from sleep he bestirred himself early, with gladness of heart, pondering in a fashion as of this world, as one who had not yet fully tasted of the Spirit of God, that he should be ere long comporting himself magnificently as a prince, and counting the vision as a presage of great prosperity, he began to plan a hasty journey to Apulia, so that he might be made a knight by the said count. And so much more gladness

5

than was usual did he manifest that to the many who marvelled and asked whence came such great joy, he answered : " I know that I am to be a great prince."

But when, after setting forth on his travels, he reached Spoleto, so that thence he might proceed towards Apulia, he was seized with a little sickness. Still, not the less anxious about his journey, when he had given himself up to sleep, he heard, while only half asleep, someone asking him whither he desired to go. When in reply he had disclosed his whole plan, the voice added : " Who is able to render thee the more good, the Lord or the servant?" When he had answered : "The Lord," the voice further said : "Why then dost thou leave the Lord for the servant, the Prince for a retainer?" And Francis said : " What dost Thou wish me to do, Lord?" "Return," said He, "to thine own country, and it shall be told thee what thou shalt do ; for the vision which thou hast seen, it behoveth thee to interpret differently."

When he awoke he began most intently to think upon this vision. And as in the first vision he had been as it were borne out of himself by great joy, while he was then desiring temporal prosperity, so in this he retired within himself entirely, marvelling at its weighty impressiveness, and pondering on it with such absorbed attention that on that night he was unable any longer to sleep.

And so when morning came he returned hastily to Assisi, glad and rejoicing to the utmost, looking for the will of the Lord, who had pointed out to him his way thus far, and trusting that the divine counsel would be given to him concerning his salvation. Being now changed in his mind, he shrank from going to Apulia, and desired to conform himself to the Divine will.

*   *   *

After he had returned to Assisi—and not many days after—on a certain evening he was chosen by his companions as master of their revels, so that he might arrange for the spending of the money devoted to their festivities, at his discretion. He accordingly then caused a rich feast to be prepared, as he had done many times before. When they had regaled themselves, they went forth from the house where they had met, and his companions in a band went on before him, singing as they went through the city, he himself carrying in his hand a wand as their master. He walked after them, just a little in their rear, not singing, but rapt in meditation.

And lo! suddenly he was visited by the Lord, and with so much sweetness was his heart filled, that he was able neither to speak nor to move,

7

and could not be conscious of anything or hear anything, but that sweetness which so alienated him from carnal sense, that, as he himself afterwards said, if he had then been sliced into pieces, he could not have stirred from the spot.

But when his companions looked behind and saw him so far away from them, turning back towards him, they in their fear took him to be as it were changed already into another man. And they questioned him, saying: "What hast thou been thinking of? Why hast thou not come up to us? Perchance thou hast been thinking of taking to thyself a wife!" He with a loud voice replied to them: "Ye have spoken truly, since I have been thinking of taking to myself a spouse, nobler, richer, and more beautiful than ever ye have seen." And they laughed at him. He however said this not of himself, but inspired by God; for that spouse was true Religion, nobler and richer and more beautiful than others in her poverty.

Thus from that hour began he to grow worthless in his own esteem, and to despise those things which aforetime he had had a fondness for; not however fully, since not yet was he entirely set free from worldly vanity. But withdrawing himself little by little from worldly confusion, he devoted himself to enshrining Jesus Christ in the inner

8

man, and to withdrawing from the eyes of the frivolous, the pearl which he, by selling all things, desired to buy.

Many times and almost every day he went secretly to prayer, constrained thereto by the said sweetness, which visiting him wherever he might be, whether in the piazza or in any place of concourse, urged him irresistibly to where he might be alone and pray.

*   *   *

Although for a long time now he had been a benefactor of the poor, nevertheless henceforth he proposed more firmly in his heart to no longer refuse alms to any poor man asking for them in God's name; but to bestow them more freely and abundantly than he had been wont to do. Therefore, always, whatever poor man asked alms from him out of doors, he supplied him with pennies, if he had any; but if he had none, he would give him a girdle, or a buckle, lest he should send the poor man empty away. But if he had none of such things, he would go to some retired place, take off his shirt, and then send the poor man there secretly, so that he might take it for himself, for the love of God.

He also would buy vessels that were necessary for the adorning of churches, and these he would send to poor priests with the utmost secrecy. But

9

when, in the absence of his father, he remained in the house, even if he alone with his mother were eating, he would cover the table with bread, as if he were preparing for the whole family. Wherefore, when asked by his mother why he placed so many loaves on the table, he would reply that he did so so that there might be alms to give to the poor, inasmuch as he purposed to give to everyone asking for alms for the love of God.

But his mother, who loved him more than she did her other sons, bore with him in such things, observing what things were done by him, and wondering much over them in her heart. For as it had been his wont to set his heart on going after his companions when he was called by them, and had been so much attracted to their society that many times he would get up from table, though he had eaten but little, leaving his parents distressed at his disappearing so unceremoniously, so now all his heart was intent upon seeing or listening to the poor on whom he might bestow alms. For so changed was he by divine grace, albeit he was still in secular attire, he desired to be in some city, where as one unknown he might divest himself of his own clothes and put on, by mutual exchange, the garments of some poor man, and so by experience know what it was to ask for alms for the love of God.

Now at that time he went to Rome on pilgrimage. And entering in the church of S. Peter,
he noticed the offerings of some that they were
small, and spoke within himself: "Inasmuch as
the Prince of the Apostles should be magnificently
honoured, why do these people make such small
offerings in the church where his body is resting?"
And so in great fervour he put his hand into his
purse and drew it out full of coins, and throwing
them through the railings of the shrine, he made
so great a noise, that at such a large offering all
who were standing by marvelled very much.
Then going outside in front of the entrance to
the church, where many poor were assembled
begging alms, he secretly bargained for the tattered
clothes of a poor little man, and laying aside his
own, he put them on, and standing on the steps
of the church with the other poor, he asked for
alms in French, since he freely spoke the French
tongue, though he knew not how to speak it
correctly.

But, afterwards, taking off the said clothes,
and putting on again his own, he returned to
Assisi, and began to pray unto the Lord that He
would direct his way. For to no one did he make
known his secret, nor in this matter did he avail
himself of the counsel of anyone, save that of God
alone, from whom he received guidance. Some-

times, however, he sought it from the bishop of
Assisi. At that time in truth, amongst none was
there true Poverty, and Poverty it was that he
desired above all things in this world, being
willing in Poverty to live and to die.

*　　*　　*

As on one day Francis was praying with
fervour unto the Lord, this answer he heard:
" Francis, all those things which thou hast loved
in fleshly way and hast longed to possess, there
is need for thee to despise and hate, if thou
wouldst have a knowledge of My will, and after
thou shalt have begun to do so, the things which
formerly seemed to thee soft and delectable will
be to thee unbearable and bitter; and from those
that thou wast wont to shrink from with dread,
thou wilt draw great sweetness and unbounded
consolation."

He was rejoicing therefore in this counsel, and
feeling strengthened in the Lord, when, as he was
riding near Assisi, he saw by the wayside one who
was a leper. And as he had been accustomed to
shrink with much alarm from lepers, he now with
an effort constrained himself, and got down from
his horse, and gave the leper a coin. Kissing his
hand, and receiving from the leper the kiss of
peace, he got again upon his horse, and proceeded
on his way. He thenceforth began more and

more to think lowlily of himself, until, by the grace of God, he over himself attained unto victory perfectly.

Then, after a few days, taking with him a large sum of money, he betook himself to the hospice for lepers. And gathering all together around him, he gave alms to each, kissing the hand too of each one. As then he went away, truly that which had aforetime been distasteful unto him—that is, to see and to touch lepers—was changed into sweetness. For, as he said, so repulsive had it been to him to have sight of lepers, that he had been unwilling not only to have sight of them, but also even to draw near to where they dwelt. And if sometimes it happened that he had to pass by their abodes, or to see them, although he would be moved by pity to bestow alms on them through anyone else, he nevertheless would always turn away his face from them, closing his nostrils with his hand. But by the grace of God he became so friendly and intimate with lepers that he would dwell amongst them and bestow on them lowly services.

*   *   *

To his comrades who still were surprised at his apparent shrinking from a soldierly enterprise, he would say that he no longer intended to go to Apulia, but that he would stay in his own country

13

and do great and noble deeds there. Such words as these induced them to ask him again and again in a jesting way: "Art thou intending, Francis, to marry a wife?" To them he replied, as he had done before, in words that would be to them but a dark parable.

*   *   *

Now a few days after, as he was walking near the church of San Damiano, the word came unto him in the Spirit that he should enter in and pray. Having entered in he began to pray fervently before a certain image of the Crucified One, which with affection and benignity spoke to him, saying: "Francis, dost thou not see that My House is falling into ruin? Go therefore and repair it for Me." And trembling and wondering he said: "Willingly will I do so, Lord." For he understood then the words to be spoken of that church of San Damiano, which from its very great antiquity was threatened with approaching ruin.

Now from that speech he was so filled with joy, and so illumined with light, that in his soul he was in all verity sensible that it was Christ Crucified who had spoken to him. Going forth from the church he found the priest thereof sitting against it, and putting his hand to his purse he offered him a certain quantity of money, saying: "I pray thee, buy oil, and let a lamp ever burn before that Crucifix; and for this purpose when this money shall have been used, I will again present unto thee as much as will then be needful."

Thus then from that hour so pierced and melted was his heart at the remembrance of the Lord's sufferings, that ever while he lived, he bore in his heart the marks of the Lord Jesus, as afterwards did most clearly appear from the renewal of the same marks in his body, marvellously wrought and most evidently shown. From that time too he afflicted himself with such great severity towards his body, that in health and in sickness, perseveringly austere to an excess as to his bodily frame, he scarcely or never was willing to be indulgent towards himself. He would abstain from food and drink, he would distress himself with tears, he would sigh as if in agony, as he meditated on the sufferings of his Divine Lord. By reason of his austerity when the day of his death was drawing nigh, he confessed that he had against his Brother Body sinned much.

*　　*　　*

These things as to his weeping and as to his abstinence are consistent with the statement that he, after the said vision, and the utterance of the Image of the Crucified One, was always, even unto his death, conformed unto the Passion of Christ.

Rejoicing at the said vision and utterance of the Crucified One, he arose, protecting himself with the sign of the cross, and mounting his horse, and taking with him stuffs of divers colours, he arrived at the city which is called Foligno. There having sold his horse and all that he had carried away, he returned directly to the church of San Damiano. He found there the poor little priest, and with great faith and devotion kissed his hands, and offered to him the money which he was carrying, and told him in an orderly narrative what his intention was.

Then the priest, surprised, and wondering at his sudden conversion, refused to believe what he told him, and thinking himself being trifled with, would not keep the money in his possession. But Francis perseveringly insisted, and strove to induce him to trust in his words, and begged the priest with even more insistence to permit him to dwell with him. The priest at last acquiesced in his tarrying with him, but from fear of Francis's parents, would not receive the money. Whereupon the true scorner of money cast it into a window, despising it as dust.

Then while he was making his abode in this place, his father was carefully enquiring what had become of his son. When he heard that he was thus changed, and where he was abiding, touched with inward grief of heart, and disturbed by what had so suddenly occurred, he called together his friends and neighbours, and hastened to his son with the utmost speed. But Francis, who was a new soldier of Christ, when he heard the threats of those who were in search of him, and saw them coming, tried to avoid conflict with his father's anger, and hastened to a certain hidden cave, which for this end he had made ready for himself. There he concealed himself for a whole month. This cave was known to one only of his father's household. There he ate in secret the food from time to time brought to him. There too he would shed a flood of tears, and pray constantly that the Lord would deliver him from hurtful persecution, and that he might be enabled, with the Lord's benignant favour, to fulfil his pious vows.

And when in fasting and in weeping he had fervently and ceaselessly besought the Lord, distrusting his own valour and persistency, his hope he cast entirely upon the Lord, who had shed upon him, although dwelling in darkness, a joy almost unutterable, and had illuminated him with a marvellous brightness. From which experience, all aglow, as was not surprising, he left his retreat, and took the road towards Assisi, hasting thither, unrestingly and joyfully.

Fortified with the arms of trust in Christ, and

kindling with a divine glow, and yet rebuking himself for inactivity and vain fear, he openly exposed himself to the hands and strokes of those who would persecute him.

They who formerly had known him, seeing him, poured upon him miserable reproaches, calling out that he was mad and out of his mind. They threw at him mud and stones. Seeing him altered from his former ways, and emaciated in body, everything that he did they set down to starvation and feeble-mindedness. But the knight of Christ passed through the midst of them all as though deaf; neither broken down by any injury nor flinching from such, he gave thanks to God.

Then when the rumour of this had gone through the piazzas and by-streets of the city, it at last reached his father. He hearing that such things were being done by his fellow-citizens, at once set forth to look for Francis, not to free him, but rather to destroy him. For with unrestrained anger, he ran as a wolf on a sheep, and looking at him with fierce eye and forbidding looks, he laid pitiless hands upon him. He dragged him into his house, and for many days shut him up in a gloomy prison, and strove with words and blows to turn back his mind to the vanity of this world.

But Francis was neither moved by words nor tired out by chains or blows, and patiently bore all things, thus becoming keener and stronger to follow out his holy purpose. On his father's leaving home, by urgent reasons of necessity, his mother, who alone remained with him, not approving of what her husband had done, spoke unto her son with soothing words. When she was not able to dissuade him from his holy purpose, the bowels of her compassion yearning over him, she broke his chains and let him go forth free. He then, rendering thanks to Almighty God, went back to the place where he had been before. Making use of a larger liberty he came forth from the wrongs he had endured freer for action and mentally braver.

In the meanwhile his father returned, and not finding his son, he, piling sins upon sins, enwrapt his wife in a whirlwind of abuse. Then he ran to the Palace of the Commune, to complain of his son before the city consuls, and to demand that they should cause to be restored to him the money which Francis had taken away. Then the consuls, seeing him thus disturbed, sent a summons by an official messenger to Francis, calling upon him to appear before them. To the messenger Francis answered, that by the grace of God he was now made free, and that the consuls had no longer any claim upon him, inasmuch as he had become the servant of the Most High God alone.

The consuls, unwilling to use force, said to his father: "Since he hath enrolled himself as a servant of God, he hath passed beyond our control." His father, seeing therefore that he could secure nothing from the consuls, brought his grievance before the bishop of the city. The bishop, discreet and wise, summoned Francis in due form to appear and reply to his father's complaint. Francis said to the bishop's messenger: "To the Lord Bishop I will come, since he is the father and lord of souls."

He came therefore to the bishop, and by him was received with great joy. To him the bishop said: "Thy father is grievously aroused against thee and greatly offended, whence if thou wishest to serve God, return to him the money which thou hast, which since perchance it hath been wrongfully gotten, God doth not wish that thou shouldst devote to the work of the Church, by reason even of the sins of thy father, whose wrath will be appeased if he receive the money back. Have, therefore, my son, trust in the Lord, and act manfully. Do not fear, for He Himself will be thine Helper, and for the needs of the Church will supply thee in abundance with what is necessary."

Then the man of God rose up rejoiced and comforted by the words of the bishop. Bringing

the money into his presence, he said to him:
"My Lord, not only the money which is his
property, do I with a cheerful mind wish to
restore to him, but even my clothes." And going
into a room of the bishop's, he stript off all his
clothes, and placing them with the money upon
them before the bishop and his father and the
others standing near, he said as he stood before
them all naked, as he had come forth from the
bishop's house: "Listen all of you, and understand. Until now I have called Peter Bernardone
my father; but since I have resolved to be a
servant of the Lord, I return him the money as
to which he was annoyed, and all the garments
which I have had from him, wishing henceforth
to say, 'Our Father which art in heaven,' not
'Father Peter Bernardone.'" Then it was found
that the man of God had worn upon his body
beneath his coloured garments a hair shirt. His
father, rising up, kindling over-much with grief
and anger, took possession of the money and of
all the clothes. As he was carrying them to his
house, they who had been present at the scene,
were indignant with him because he had left none
of the clothing for his son. Moved with true pity
for Francis they began to weep abundantly.

Then the bishop, taking earnest heed of the
mind of the man of God, and marvelling at his

fervour and constancy, threw his arms around him and flung over him his cloak. For he clearly understood that his doings had been prompted by Divine counsel, and recognised that what he had seen was the outward appearance of a not small mystery. So henceforward he became his helper, exhorting, cherishing, and directing him, and enfolding him with heartfelt love.

*   *   *

Therefore did Francis, the servant of God, disrobed of all things which are of this world, leave himself open to the influence of Divine justice, and thinking little of ordinary life, set himself free in every way possible for Divine service. Returning to the church of San Damiano, full of joy and fervour, he made for himself a dress somewhat like unto a hermit's, and encouraged the priest of that church with the same words wherewith he himself had been encouraged by the bishop.

Then he arose and went back into the city, and began, as though inebriated with the Spirit, to sing the Lord's praises through the piazzas and streets. When he had thus praised the Lord, he turned himself to the work of gathering stones for the repair of the said church, saying: "Whosoever shall give me one stone shall have one reward; but whosoever shall give two, shall have two

rewards ; and whosoever shall give three, shall
have rewards the same in number." These and
many other simple words he spoke in the fervour
of the Spirit. As a foolish and simple one, chosen
of God, not using learned words of human wisdom,
but in all things manifesting simplicity, did he
comport himself.

Many derided him, thinking he was mad, but
others, aroused to pity, were moved to tears,
seeing that he had been transformed quickly
from extreme worldly frivolity and vanity, so as
to be filled with the enthusiasm of Divine love.
But he, thinking nought of all deridings, in fervour
of spirit gave thanks unto God.

How much he toiled in the aforesaid work, it
would be long and difficult to narrate. For he
who had been accustomed to such ease in his
father's house, bore the stones on his own shoulders,
bringing distress upon himself in many ways in
his toil for God. But the priest of San Damiano,
knowing that Francis had been daintily nurtured,
began by providing for him richly-made dishes
and tempting morsels. When, however, he became
aware of what the priest was doing for him,
Francis spoke thus to himself : " Wilt thou find
this priest wherever thou shalt go, to provide for
thee such kindnesses ? This is not the life of a
poor man, which thou didst intend to adopt. But

as a poor man, going from door to door, carrieth in his hand his dish, and, compelled by need, gathereth into it divers sorts of food, thus it behoveth thee voluntarily to live for the love of Him who was born poor, and who lived in this world in the poorest way, and remained naked and poor upon the cross, and was buried in the tomb of another."

Wherefore, on an early day, he took a dish and went into the city, there begging alms from door to door, and when he had put into his bowl various sorts of food, many, who knew that he had lived so daintily before, marvelled when they saw him so wonderfully transformed as to have such contempt for himself. But when he would have eaten those mingled scraps, he at first shrank from doing so, since he had never been wont to eat, or even to see, such food. At last, however, conquering himself, he began to eat, and it seemed to him that no delicacy had ever seemed so delightful. Henceforth his heart rejoiced in God that his flesh, although feeble and afflicted, was made strong to endure with gladness whatever was harsh and bitter, for the Lord's sake. Therefore he gave God thanks that for him He had changed bitter into sweet, and had bestowed upon him manifold consolations.

He continued to toil devotedly and perseveringly both to complete the reparation of the church and to procure gifts to enable this to be accomplished, and also to obtain oil so that the sacred lamps might be kept brightly burning.

When the work of restoring the church of San Damiano was finished, the Blessed Francis was wearing, as was his wont, the garment of a hermit, and walked forth, carrying in his hand a staff, and with his feet sandalled and tied with thongs. But he heard one day at Holy Communion the words which Christ spoke unto His disciples as He was sending them forth to preach, forsooth that they should take with them on the way neither gold nor silver, nor purse nor wallet, nor bread, nor staff, and have neither sandals nor two tunics. When he understood afterwards more clearly from the same priest the import of these same words, he was filled with unutterable joy. " This," said he, " is what I desire with my utmost strength to carry out."

Therefore, having committed to memory all that he had listened to, he strove to fulfil the command with gladness. Without delay, whatever he had two of he threw aside one. Staff, sandals, purse, wallet—henceforth he did not use. He made for himself a rough and forlorn looking tunic. Throwing away his leathern belt, he girded himself with a rope. He thus began by divine impulse to be a herald of Gospel perfection, and to be an open-air preacher of repentance, speaking ever in words of simplicity.

For his words were not empty ones, or deserving of ridicule, but full of the Holy Spirit, piercing to the marrow of the heart, so that his listeners were carried away by him in wonder. As he himself afterwards testified, he began his teaching, as the Lord had revealed unto him, with this salutation, " The Lord give thee peace." He thus in all his preaching announced peace in his opening words. And as he heralded peace, and preached salvation, many who had been in heart severed from Christ, and far removed from salvation, became by Francis's wholesome exhortations brought into union with true peace.

The simple teaching of the Blessed Francis and the influence of his life so simple, gradually made an abiding impress upon many. Two years after his conversion, certain men, moved by his teaching, and won by his example, began to turn towards higher things, and attached themselves to him in the same life of devotion.

II. SAINT FRANCIS AND HIS FIRST COMPANIONS.

It must be made known that our Blessed Father Francis was in all his actions conformed to Christ. For as Christ the Blessed in the commencement of His preaching chose to Himself twelve Apostles, who left all for Him, so the Blessed Francis had twelve chosen companions, all devoted to the deepest poverty.

The first one chosen was Bernard of the Five Valleys. He was of great influence in Assisi. He was of a family of much repute. He was endued with wondrous prudence, and before his call was very rich in this world's goods.

The second one was Peter of Catania, who along with Bernard was led by the example of Saint Francis to the adoption of evangelic poverty. Bernard and Peter both attached themselves to the life of lowliness, and to the end of their lives continued in that life patiently aiming at Gospel perfection.

The third companion was Giles. He was chosen about eight days after Bernard and Peter had entered upon the new life and had distributed their possessions to the poor. Giles, seeing how these noble knights of Assisi despised earthly things, so that all around marvelled, glowing with a divine fervour, went early on the Feast of S. George to the church of S. Gregory, and after he had offered up his prayers went on to the hospital for lepers, where Saint Francis and Brother Bernard and Brother Peter were dwelling in humility most profound. Coming unto a parting of the ways, he knew not which path to take. He prayed to Christ, the loving Guide, who led him by the right way, to the hut which was the lowly hospital. As he was meditating on the purpose for which he had come, Saint Francis, who had come into the wood close by to pray, drew nigh to him. Brother Giles sank down on his knees before Saint Francis, and entreated him for the love of God to receive him into his little band. Saint Francis, looking into the earnest face of Giles, said : " My brother most dear, God hath given thee abundant grace. If the emperor were to come to Assisi, and offer to make some one of its citizens his knight or chamberlain, would not such a one be greatly joyful? How much more shouldst thou be full of joy that God hath

28

called thee to be His knight and trusted servant, to live the perfect life of His holy Gospel! Do thou therefore continue steadfast in the life to which God hath called thee." He then took him by the hand and raised him up, and led him into the hut, and called Brother Bernard, and said: "God hath sent us a good brother; let us, therefore, rejoice in the Lord, and eat with one another in charity." And when they had eaten, Francis and Giles went to Assisi to obtain cloth for a habit for the new companion.

Saint Francis speedily set forth with Giles on a mission journey to various towns near Ancona, and sent at the same time Bernard and Peter to other northern towns. Later on they all returned to the humble hut. Then a fourth companion presented himself. This was Sabbatini.

The fifth companion was Morico, who at the time of his call was one of the order of Cross-bearers. He had been sick, and nigh unto death, but by the prayers and ministrations of Saint Francis was restored to health. He then attached himself to Saint Francis, and became noted for austerity of life. But though severe in his self-denial, he was rewarded henceforth with perfect health and strength.

The sixth one to attach himself to Saint Francis was John of the Chapel; but alas! this one was in the end unfaithful and died the death of remorse and despair.

For a while Saint Francis dwelt with the brotherhood in a lonely hermitage on a rocky height overlooking the valley of Rieti. They gave themselves up to meditation and prayer, and to the instruction and edification of many who flocked around them, drawn by what they had heard of the holiness of the little company. Thus it was that the seventh companion was attracted to the brotherhood. This was Philip the Long. On his being received, Saint Francis returned to the lepers' hut, and all his companions with him.

The eighth, ninth, and tenth of the companions of Saint Francis were Constantius, or John of S. Constantius; Barbarus; and Bernard of Viridant, or Vigilantius. Of these the deeds and utterances are unknown.

A certain priest, Sylvester by name, saw that Saint Francis was wont to give much money to the poor. A feeling of avarice took possession of him, and he said to Saint Francis: "Thou hast not given me enough for the stones I sold thee for the repair of the church. Now that thou hast money, pay me what thou owest." Thereupon Saint Francis, much wondering at the demand, but, wishing to be guided by the precepts of the

Gospel, thrust his hand between the folds of the dress of Bernard, who was standing near, and drew out a handful of money. This he gave to Sylvester, telling him that if he wanted more he should have it. Sylvester was contented, and returned home. But during the evening hours he bethought himself of his avarice, and of Bernard's zeal, and of the holiness of Saint Francis. He saw in a vision Saint Francis, and from the saint's mouth there seemed to come forth a cross, which reached up to heaven, and stretched forth its arms far away eastwards and westwards. Because of this vision, he gave, from love to God, all that he was possessed of to the poor, and joined the brotherhood of Saint Francis. He lived a life of such holiness, and was so favoured with especial graces, that he had converse with God as a friend with a friend. Sylvester was the eleventh companion of Saint Francis.

The twelfth companion was Angelo Tancredi of Rieti. He was a knight, gentle and courteous, noble both by birth and by character. It was at Rieti that Saint Francis met him. He greeted him by his name, as though he had long known him. He said : "Angelo, long enough hast thou worn thy sword and thy belt. The time hath come for thee to have a thick cord instead of thy belt ; the cross of Jesus instead of thy sword ; mud and

31

dust on thy feet instead of thy spurs. Follow me, therefore, and of thee I will make a soldier of Jesus Christ." The knight obeyed the call, forsook his knightly pursuits, and was soon garbed as a companion of Saint Francis.

After the sad withdrawal of John of the Chapel, another was chosen in his place. It was at Rome that Saint Francis, by his fervent preaching, so influenced a listener that he felt constrained to seek to be numbered amongst the evangelic band. The listener was not a Roman, not even an Italian, but an Englishman. So that henceforth one of English birth and with the English name of William, was deemed to be the twelfth companion of Saint Francis.

* * *

Our Father Francis had cast all his thought upon Christ the Blessed One, and ordered all studies and all desires as to praying and preaching on the part both of himself and his companions to be such as would be well pleasing unto Christ. When in the beginning of his conversion, on a certain occasion the pious father sat with his sons so blessed, in fervour of spirit he enjoined one of them in the name of the Lord to open his mouth, and speak of God whatever the Holy Spirit suggested to him. But when he without delay and with obedience began, and, at the teaching of the Holy Spirit, gave utterance to thoughts of surprising power, the blessed father imposed silence on him and bade another that he should, in like manner, speak of God, according to the grace by the Holy Spirit bestowed upon him. And he being obedient and pouring forth by divine grace great things of God, Saint Francis upon him, as upon the first, imposed silence. And a third he ordered that, to the praise of the Lord Jesus Christ, he should, without premeditation, utter some thoughts. And this third, by the example of the others, and humbly fulfilling obedience, brought forward into light such marvels and subtleties as to the hidden things of God, that in no one was there doubt that by him as by the others the Holy Spirit had spoken.

When therefore they thus one by one had from the vase of holy simplicity poured forth the balsam of divine grace—for each at the bidding of the holy father had spoken mellifluously of divine things—lo! in their midst appeared the Lord Jesus Christ, in the likeness of a radiant youth, blessing all with such gracious sweetness, that the holy father as well as the others were rapt in ecstasy, and fell upon the ground as though bereft of life, utterly unconscious of anything of this world. But when they returned to themselves, the holy father said : " My brethren most beloved, give thanks to the Lord Jesus Christ, because it hath pleased Him by the mouths of simple ones to scatter celestial treasures. He who openeth the mouths of babes and of mutes maketh, when He will, the tongues of the simple to be wise and eloquent."

To the praise of God.

III. SAINT FRANCIS AND BROTHER BERNARD OF THE FIVE VALLEYS.

Brother Bernard, the first and the first-born of Saint Francis's companions both as to priority of time and as to saintly endowments, was converted thus. Francis was still in secular attire, though he had given up all worldly hopes and was held in no esteem, and by reason of being absorbed in penitential and mortifying experiences was thought by many not to be in his right mind. He was however seasoned with divine salt, and by the Holy Spirit established and confirmed in tranquillity; and thus for a long time when he passed through the streets of Assisi, he received unnumbered injuries from the mud and stones thrown at him both by his own kindred and by strangers; but he was very patient and passed along with cheerful countenance, deaf to words of insult and keeping silent amid provocation.

Now Bernard of Assisi who was one of the noblest and richest and wisest of the whole city, in whose counsels all acquiesced, began to observe with deep pondering the profound contempt of the world there was in Saint Francis, and how great was his constancy amid the injuries inflicted on him, and how great his patience in enduring them, so that although for almost two years he had been hated and scorned by men, he ever seemed the more steadfast. Bernard said in his heart: "This Francis cannot be other than one who hath received largely of the grace of God."

Inspired by God he invited Saint Francis to an evening meal. Saint Francis humbly consented. But Bernard had set his heart upon seeing evidences of the sanctity of the Blessed Francis. Wherefore he asked him to rest that night in his house. This Saint Francis submissively assented to. Bernard caused to be made ready for him a bed in his own room, in which a lamp was kept burning all night. Saint Francis, as soon as he came within the room, so that he might hide from view the divine grace which abode with him, threw himself on the bed, apparently as though wishing to sleep. Bernard too sought repose, and speedily feigned to be sleeping soundly.

Saint Francis, a faithful screener of the secrets of God, when he thought that Bernard was in deep sleep, in the profound silence of the night, arose from his bed. Looking heavenwards, and lifting up hands and eyes towards God with earnestness and fervour, he prayed most devoutly: "My God and my all!" And with tears he kept on till morning, uttering no other words than these: "My God and my all!"

This Saint Francis said, marvelling at the excellence of the Divine Majesty which seemed to descend to a world in peril, and by the Divine Son to offer salvation to all. For, enlightened by the spirit of prophecy, he foresaw the great things which God would do through his Order, and by the teaching of the same spirit considering his own insufficiency and his little worth, he entreated the Lord that what he himself could not do, should be done by Divine power, without which human weakness can do nothing. After which he prayed: "My God and my all!"

Bernard, by the shining of the lamp, having seen the devotion of the Saint, and having pondered over the words that had been uttered, and being prompted by the Holy Spirit, in the early morning called Saint Francis, and said to him: "Brother Francis, I have inwardly resolved to quit the world, and in whatsoever thou mayst command me, to follow thee." Saint Francis, hearing these words, rejoiced in spirit and with great gladness said: "Bernard, what thou hast spoken of is a work so arduous that as to it counsel must be sought of our Lord Jesus Christ, that He may deign to show us His goodwill as to how we ought to bring it about. So let us go with one another to the bishop's house, where there is a good priest; let us attend Holy Communion, and then we will pray until the hour of tierce. In our prayer we will seek this from the Lord Jesus Christ, that He will deign to show us in three openings of the Missal the way most pleasing to Himself that we ought to choose." Bernard said: "What thou sayest pleaseth me."

They went therefore to the bishop's house, and after Holy Communion and prayer prolonged until tierce, the priest, at the request of Saint Francis and Bernard, took the service book. Reverently making the sign of the cross, he opened the Gospels, in the name of our Lord Jesus Christ. At the opening the words ran: "If thou wilt be perfect, go and sell that thou hast and give to the poor." At the second opening the passage ran: "Whosoever will come after Me, let him deny himself and take up his cross and follow Me." At the third opening, the words were: "Ye shall take nothing for the journey." Having seen these words, Saint Francis said to Bernard: "Lo! we have the Lord's counsel. Go and act out what thou hast heard. Blessed be our Lord Jesus Christ, who hath deigned to point out to us the Gospel pathway."

Bernard at once sold all his possessions, which were of great value, and distributed all to the poor. Carrying a lapful of money to widows, orphans, pilgrims, and to God's ministers, he distributed to them affluently and liberally. Saint Francis went with him and helped him faithfully in all the aforesaid distribution.

Bernard having dispersed all his goods for the Lord's sake, and having in all things made himself poor Gospel-wise, was enriched with so great favour from God that he was often caught up to the Lord's presence. Saint Francis pronounced him worthy of all reverence, and declared that he was the very founder of the Order, since he by giving his all to the poor was the first to embrace evangelical poverty, reserving nothing at all for himself, and offering himself stript of everything to the arms of the Crucified One, who is blessed for ever. Amen.

*   *   *

What abundant grace the Father Most High often granted to the poor followers of the Gospel, who for the love of Christ voluntarily forsook all things, is shown in Brother Bernard, who after he had donned the habit of Saint Francis was many times rapt in God through contemplation of things celestial. It chanced once that when in a church, giving attentive heed to the holy mysteries, and with his whole mind lifted up towards things divine, he was so absorbed in God that at the sacramental elevation of the body of Christ, he thereof saw nothing; neither did he kneel; nor did he withdraw his hood, as did the others who were there; but without the slightest blinking of his eyes, he remained gazing fixedly, and with senses all asleep he thus remained from matins until nones. But after nones, coming back to himself, he passed on through the church, crying with voice of wonder: "O brothers! O brothers! O brothers! there is no one in this land so great or so noble to whom if there were promised a palace filled with gold would not eagerly carry there a sack full of dung to win that treasure so noble!"

To that celestial treasure, for lovers of God reserved, was Brother Bernard so uplifted in thought that for fifteen years right onward he ever went with mind and countenance raised to heaven, and in that time never did he appease his hunger at table, although he ate a little of what was placed before him. For he said that as to what a man did not taste he could not be abstinent, but that true abstinence is being temperate in the things that are pleasant to the taste.

To such great clearness and luminousness of

intellect did he arrive that even great clerics resorted to him for the solving of hard questions and of dark passages of Scripture, and he made clear every difficulty for them. And inasmuch as his mind was entirely free and set loose from earthly things, he, as a swallow, flew on high by contemplation, and sometimes for twenty days, and sometimes for thirty days, he hovered alone over the summits of loftiest mountains, contemplating things celestial. For which Brother Giles said of him that there was not given to other men this gift bestowed on Brother Bernard of the Five Valleys, by which he was wont as a swallow to feed in flight. By reason of this grace so excellent, received from God, Saint Francis willingly and often spoke with him by day and by night. Sometimes they were found to have been together all night through, rapt in God, in the forest where they had met, they twain, to converse of the Lord Jesus Christ, of Him who is blessed for ever. Amen.

*   *   *

The most devout servant of Christ the Crucified One, Francis, by reason of the severity of his penitential discipline and continual weeping, had made himself almost blind, so that he could see but little.

Upon a certain time he withdrew from a place

where he had been, and proceeded to where Bernard had been lingering. Bernard was standing in a wood, in contemplation divine, wholly drawn from earth, and lost in union with God. Then Saint Francis advanced into the wood and called to Brother Bernard, saying: "Come, speak to this blind man of thine!" But Brother Bernard, as he was a man of deep contemplativeness, and was then lifted up in mind towards God, did not respond to Saint Francis, or go to him. Brother Bernard was possessed of a singular grace in speaking of God. Blessed Francis had many times himself experienced this, and so had the greater desire to speak with him. Therefore after a little while he called him a second time, and a third time, repeating the same words: "Come, speak to this blind man of thine!" Neither time did Brother Bernard take notice, and neither went nor spoke to Saint Francis. So that Saint Francis retreated a little, disconsolate, wondering and almost grieving that Brother Bernard thrice called by him should be unwilling to go to him.

Saint Francis, thus thinking, as he went away said to the companion with him: "Wait for me a little while." And as he gave himself up to prayer in a solitary place, a divine response was made to him: "Wherefore art thou, O poor little

man, troubled? Ought a man to leave God for
any creature? Brother Bernard, when thou didst
call him, was in communion with Me, and therefore could not come to thee, or reply to thee.
Wherefore do not marvel if he could not speak
to thee, since he was so uplifted that thy words
he heard not at all."

Saint Francis being thus enlightened, at once
with great speed returned to Brother Bernard
that he might humbly accuse himself of the
thought that had lodged in his mind. But
Brother Bernard, truly holy, saw Saint Francis
approach, and straightway ran towards him, and
cast himself at his feet. The humility of Saint
Francis and the love and reverence of Brother
Bernard met together. Having recited the divine
reprimand which he had received, Saint Francis
commanded Brother Bernard that whatever he
should enjoin upon him that he should do for
obedience sake. But he fearing lest Saint Francis
should impose upon himself something too bur-
densome, as he was wont to do, wished to avoid
the pious obedience, and said: "Ready I am, my
father, to act out thy obedience, if only thou wilt
promise me obedience as to what I will tell thee
of." "I assent," replied Saint Francis. Brother
Bernard then said: "Tell me, my father, what
thou wishest me to do." Then Saint Francis

43

said: "By holy obedience I bid thee, in order to punish the presumption and forwardness of my heart, when I cast myself on the ground, that thou tread with one foot upon my throat, and with the other upon my mouth, and thus thrice walk over me from one side to the other. Thus passing over me, thou shalt utter reproaches, 'Lie there, thou restless rustic son of Peter Bernardone.' And many other and greater slights thou shalt inflict on me, in these words, 'Whence is thy so great pride, thou who art so worthless a creature?'"

Hearing which, Brother Bernard shrank from doing what to him was hard. Yet, for obedience, he began even with what courtliness he could put forth, to fulfil the behest. After it was done, Saint Francis said: "Now, Brother Bernard, utter thy command, since I have promised obedience to thee." But Brother Bernard said: "By holy obedience, I bid thee whensoever we are together, by reason of my failings, to correct and sharply reprove me." Hearing which, Saint Francis was much astonished, since Brother Bernard was of such deep sanctity that Saint Francis held him in great reverence.

Wherefore from that time Saint Francis feared to linger with him very long, by reason of the promised obedience, lest he might be on the verge of assailing a mind so holy and so divine with

any correction. But when he desired to see
Brother Bernard, or listen to him as he spoke of
God, he withdrew from him swiftly and abruptly.
And it was marvellous to see how in the reverend
father and in the first-born son, forsooth, Brother
Bernard, there contended together, yea rather
met together, the obedience and the love, the
patience and the humility, of both.

To the praise and glory of God.

*   *   *

Seeing that our Blessed Father Francis had
been himself called by the Lord from the Cross
and to the Cross, both he and his first companions seemed and were as men crucified. That
they bore the Cross was seen in their habit, in
their simple life, and in all their deeds. Reproaches such as Christ endured they desired
more than the vain and delusive blandishments
of the world. Wherefore insults made them glad,
and honours saddened them. They went through
the world as pilgrims and strangers bearing
about with them nothing but Christ Crucified.
So that, wherever they went, as they were living
branches of the true Vine, they produced great
and good spiritual fruit—the souls they won
for God.

It happened in the early days of the Order
that Saint Francis sent Brother Bernard to

Bologna, that there he might produce fruit for God according to the grace given to him by the Lord. Whereupon Brother Bernard, making the sign of the Cross of Christ, and by virtue of holy obedience, went to Bologna.

When the street-boys saw him in his garb so strange and wretched, they began to insult him as though he were a witless man. But Brother Bernard bore these insults, not only with patience, but even with the utmost joy. For because he was truly a disciple of Christ, who was despised and rejected of men, for the love of Him he went and stood in the market-place of the city, with the intent that he might be the more reviled. While he was sitting there, many boys and men gathered around him. They snatched at his hood, some from behind and others in front of him. Some threw dust at him; others stones. Some pushed him heavily one way, some another.

And Brother Bernard continued joyful and patient amid all these insults, in no way resisting or murmuring; and indeed, what is more to be observed, he purposely returned for several days, one after the other, to the said market-place, to endure the like treatment. Whatsoever ill-usage he received, he was always with mind undisturbed and with face full of joy.

And since patience ever accomplishes perfect

work, and is a proof of virtue, a wise teacher of the law, taking note of and pondering over the brave constancy in no wise unsettled during so many days, said in his heart: "Impossible it is that this is not a holy man." Approaching Brother Bernard, he said: "Who art thou, and wherefore dost thou come hither?" Brother Bernard thrust his hand into his bosom and brought forth the rule of Saint Francis—the rule which he carried in his heart and which he showed forth by his deeds. He, when he had read it, and had thought well upon its lofty standard of perfection, with great amazement and admiration, turned to his companions and said: "Truly this is the highest standard of religion that I have ever heard of. Wherefore this man and his associates are amongst the holiest men of the world, and whoso doeth him a wrong sinneth greatly; for he ought to be held in highest honour, as a great friend of God."

He said to Brother Bernard: "If I could find for thee a suitable house, where thou mightest fittingly serve God, I, for the salvation of my soul, would freely give such to thee." Brother Bernard replied: "I believe that our Lord Jesus Christ hath breathed this thought into thy mind, and thine offer I accept with willingness for the honour of Christ."

Then the said judge, with great delight and

love, led Brother Bernard to his house, and afterwards bestowed upon him the promised house, which he made fit for use and furnished at his own cost; and from that time forth he became the special patron and defender of Brother Bernard and his companions. Brother Bernard, by means of his holy conversation, began to be much honoured, and so greatly so, that they counted themselves happy who could touch him and listen to his words or have a glimpse of him.

But Brother Bernard, as truly a humble disciple of Christ and of the humble Saint Francis, fearing lest the honour there bestowed upon him might endanger his peace and salvation, withdrew, and returning to Saint Francis, spoke thus to him: "Father, there is a house established in the city of Bologna. Send brethren there to carry it on and dwell therein, since I can no longer gain advantage there. On the contrary, by reason of the too great honour rendered to me I fear that I have lost there more than I have gained." Then Saint Francis, hearing of all things in order, how that God had worked through Brother Bernard, rejoicing and exulting in spirit, began to praise the Most High, who thus had begun to add to the number of the poor little disciples of the Cross. He afterwards sent some of his companions to Bologna and to Lombardy,

who established houses in divers places, aided
therein by the increasing devotion of faithful ones.
To the praise and honour of the good Jesus.

*   *   *

Of such sanctity was Brother Bernard, that
Saint Francis, while he lived, had a great vene-
ration for him, commended him in frequent
utterances, and in his absence extolled him with
exceeding laudation. It happened that while
Saint Francis on a certain day was persevering
devoutly in prayer, it was revealed to him that
Brother Bernard, with divine consent, would be
assailed very grievously by many evil spirits.

Whilst Saint Francis was pondering with compassionate mind upon his son so beloved, through
many days with tearful prayers, he commended
Brother Bernard to the Lord Jesus Christ, that
he would deign to give him victory in the midst
of so many snares. And whilst Saint Francis
was thus praying, watchfully, anxiously, intently,
lo! there was made to him a divine response:
" Brother, fear not, since all temptations with
which Brother Bernard is assailed are given to
him for the discipline which leadeth to the crown
of perfection, and finally over all his foes he will
gain victory and victory's reward with joy. Brother
Bernard is indeed one of those who will enter
into the fellowship of the kingdom of God."

With which response Saint Francis rejoiced with great joy, and gave thanks unnumbered to the Lord Jesus Christ. And from that time he had no more doubts or fears as to Bernard, but loved him ever with a greater joy and a more embracing affection. This affection he displayed not only in life, but also in the hour of death.

For, when dying, like as with the patriarch Jacob, while his sons were standing by in tearful devotion at the departure of so lovable a father, Saint Francis said: "Where is my first-born? Come, my son, that my soul may bless thee before I die."

Then Brother Bernard spoke in an under-tone to Brother Elias, who was the Vicar of the Order, and said: "Father, go to the right of the Saint, that he may bless thee." When Brother Elias placed himself at the right hand, and Saint Francis, almost blind by reason of his many tears, had put his right hand upon the head of Elias, he said: "This is not the head of my first-born, Brother Bernard."

Then Brother Bernard drew nigh to his left. But Saint Francis then arranged his arms cross-wise, and put his right hand upon the head of Brother Bernard, and his left hand upon the head of Brother Elias, and said to Brother Bernard: "May the Father of my Lord Jesus

Christ bless thee with every spiritual blessing in
celestial things in Christ. As thou art the first
one chosen in this Order to give an evangelic
example, and to imitate Christ in Gospel poverty,
seeing that not only what was thine own didst
thou offer freely, and for the love of Christ didst
entirely distribute it, but also hast offered thyself
to God as a sacrifice with the odour of sweetness,
therefore blessed be thou by the Lord Jesus
Christ and by myself, His poor little servant, with
eternal blessings, coming and going, waking and
sleeping, living and dying. Whoso shall bless
thee, may he be filled with blessings, and whoso
shall curse thee, may he be fittingly requited.
Be thou lord of thy brethren, and may all sub-
mit to thy rule. And whomsoever thou shalt
wish to receive into this Order, they shall be
received; and whomsoever thou shalt wish to
dismiss, they shall be dismissed. And no one of
the brethren shall have power over thee, and
wheresoever thou shalt wish to go or to remain,
thou shalt freely have thy wish."

Now when this son so blessed, himself drew
nigh unto death, inasmuch as the brethren after
the dying of Saint Francis venerated him with
affection as a father, from various parts of the
world many came to him. Amongst whom was
the angelic and divine Brother Giles, who when

he saw Brother Bernard, said to him with great joy: "Lift up your heart! Brother Bernard! lift up your heart!" Brother Bernard spoke to a brother in an under-tone that he should get ready a place meet for contemplation, where Brother Giles might muse upon heavenly things.

And when Brother Bernard had arrived at the last hour before his departure hence, he caused himself to be raised up, and said to the brethren standing nigh: "Dearest brothers, I will not speak to you many words, but wish you to think of this, that the state of life which hath been mine you still have as yours, and that what befalleth me now will in the future befall you. And I find this in my mind that for a thousand worlds like unto this, I would not have done other than serve our Lord Jesus Christ. And for every fault that I have committed, I accuse myself before my Divine Saviour, my Lord Jesus Christ, and before you. I pray you, brothers of mine most beloved, that ye love one another."

After these words and other wholesome exhortations, when he had fallen back upon his bed, his face became resplendent and full of joy, and all around marvelled thereat. In this joy, his soul, happy with the victory before promised to himself, passed to the gladness of the blessed.

To the praise of God.

IV. SAINT FRANCIS AND BROTHER PETER.

So that he might observe the virtue of holy humility, Saint Francis, when a few years had slipped by after his conversion, in a certain chapter, in the presence of the brethren, resigned the office of Superior, saying: "From this time I am dead to you; but see here Brother Peter of Catania, unto whom I and you will all be obedient." And prostrating himself on the ground, he promised obedience and reverence unto the same.

Thereupon all the brethren wept, and very great sorrow did wring forth deep laments, when forsooth they saw themselves in a manner become orphans to such a father. But the blessed father rising up, and with his eyes lifted up towards heaven and with his hands joined, said: "Lord, I commend to Thee this family, whom Thou hast hitherto entrusted to me, and now, by reason of the weakness of which Thou knowest,

O Lord, most sweet, not being able to keep them in my care, I give them into the care of the ministers. These shall be required in the day of judgment, before Thee, O Lord, to render account, if perchance, by reason of their negligence or ill example, or unloving correction, any one of them shall have perished."

He remained therefore henceforth subject unto others, even until his death, in all things more humbly bearing himself than any of the others.

V. SAINT FRANCIS AND BROTHER GILES.

In the first days of the Religion whilst Saint Francis was dwelling at Rivo Torto with the two whom he then only had as companions, lo a certain one, Giles by name, who was the third brother, came from the world to him, so that he might enter upon his way of life.

And whilst he thus remained there for some days wearing the attire he had brought from the world, it chanced that a certain poor man came to that house seeking alms from the Blessed Francis. The Blessed Francis turned to Giles and said to him: "Give the poor brother thy mantle." He at once with great joy took it from his back, and gave it to the poor man. And then it seemed to him that God had forthwith sent new grace into his heart, since with gladness he had given the mantle to the poor man. And so having then been received by the Blessed Francis, ever did he bravely advance towards highest perfection.

VI. BROTHER GILES AND SAINT LOUIS.

When Saint Louis, king of France, had resolved upon his septennial pilgrimage to Christian sanctuaries, and had heard the report of the sanctity of holy Brother Giles, he determined in his heart by all means to visit him. Wherefore in his pilgrimage diverging to Perugia, where he had heard that Brother Giles was dwelling, he came to the gate of the brethren's house as a poor and unknown pilgrim, with few companions, and asked very pressingly for Brother Giles, saying nothing to the porter as to who it was who made the request. The porter went and told Brother Giles that a pilgrim was asking for him at the gate. But at once by the Spirit he recognised who it was. As though overcome with joy, he left his cell and ran with the swiftest speed to the gate. They both fell into each other's arms, embracing each other wonderingly, and kissing one another in devout salutation, and then knelt down with one another; acting as if in ancient friendship they had known one another before. And having manifested these signs of love to one another, each to the other not uttering a word, but in every way mutually keeping silence, they separated from one another.

BROTHER GILES AND SAINT LOUIS

But when Saint Louis had withdrawn, one of his companions was asked by the brethren who it was who had thrown himself into such an affectionate embrace with Brother Giles. He replied that it was Louis, king of France, who as he was proceeding on pilgrimage wished to see the holy Brother Giles. Then the brethren spoke in lamenting tones to Brother Giles, and said: "O Brother Giles, wherefore, to so great a king, who came from France to see thee and hear from thee some good word, hast thou been content to say nothing?" Brother Giles replied: "Dearest brothers, do not wonder, if neither he to me nor I to him could say a single word; for, as soon as we had embraced, the light of divine wisdom revealed his heart to me and my heart to him. And as though we both stood looking into a mirror of transcendent kind, whatsoever he thought to say to me, or I to him, we heard, without noise of lip or tongue, with clear consoling effect, better than if we had spoken with the lips. If we had wished to unfold the things which we inwardly felt, by the ministry of vocal sound, speech itself would have tended rather to bewilder than to console us. Know accordingly that the king departed wonderfully comforted."

VII.   SAINT   FRANCIS   AND
BROTHER   ELIAS.

The most Blessed Father Francis as he was devoutly praying revoked the sentence of God against a sinner, as was clear in the case of Brother Elias, who was the second general minister after the Blessed Francis.

For when the apostasy of Brother Elias himself from the Order and the Church, and his condemnation, were revealed to the Blessed Francis, he by reason of this altogether shunned Brother Elias to such an extent that he neither would walk along the way on which Brother Elias might be, nor would look at him or speak with him or have any communication with him. Brother Elias pondering upon this, asked the Blessed Francis why he so avoided him.   The Blessed Francis replied and told him that he was a lost one, and would apostatize.   Hearing which, Brother Elias, altogether softened into tears, cast himself down at the feet of the Blessed Francis, and said: " For me, thy sheep,

I beseech thee that thou wilt pray unto God; for I trust so much in thy prayers that if I were in deepest hell and thou wert to pray to God for me, I should feel some solace, all the more because God knoweth how to alter His judgment if man turn away from his wrong-doing. Pray therefore to God for me."

Our Blessed Father Saint Francis, moved by the tears of Brother Elias, betook himself to prayer for him, and as he prayed was hearkened to by God. And he told Brother Elias that he would not come under condemnation, but that he would indeed quit the Order. Thus it happened; for Brother Elias being deposed from the office of General of the Order by Lord Gregory the Ninth, Albert of Pisa, then minister in England, being chosen in his place, joined himself unto the Emperor Frederick. On account of which he was excommunicated by the Pope, and deprived of the habit of the Order. But Brother Elias being in Sicily and feeling ill, his brother according to the flesh, who was a Brother Minor and a lay brother, having obtained permission went to visit him in Sicily. And finding him very infirm he caused that Brother Elias should acknowledge his error and should write a letter to the Pope.

This letter that brother carried to the Pope,

59

and from him obtained the concession that Elias should be pardoned and clothed again in the habit of the Order. And then the brother returned to Elias, whom he found still living. So that Brother Elias was set free from the excommunication, and reclothed in the habit of the Order, and having received the Sacraments of the Church he ended his life in peace, restored to spiritual health by the prayer and the influence of the merits of the Blessed Francis.

VIII. SAINT FRANCIS AND
BROTHER LEO.

Once in the winter time Saint Francis was
going from Perugia to Saint Mary of the Angels.
There was with him Brother Leo. The cold was
excruciatingly bitter to them. Saint Francis
called to Brother Leo, who was going on a little
before him, and said: "O Brother Leo, although
the Brothers Minor give a great example of
holiness and uprightness and good edification,
nevertheless, write, that is, take heed diligently,
that not there is perfect joy."

And when he had walked on a little further,
Saint Francis called to him again, saying: "O
Brother Leo, although a Brother Minor should
give the blind sight, give to the crooked straight-
ness, chase away evil spirits, give to the deaf
hearing, make the lame to walk, and to the dumb
restore speech, and, what is more, should give
life to one who had been four days dead, write,
that not therein is perfect joy." And again crying out, he said: "O Brother Leo, if a Brother
Minor should know all nations' tongues, and all

sciences and scriptures, so that he should be able to foretell and unveil not only the things of the future, but even the inner consciences of others, write, that herein is not perfect joy."

And as they still went on walking, he again cried: "O Brother Leo, God's lamblike one, although a Brother Minor should speak angelic tongues and know the courses of the stars, and the healing virtues of herbs, and though the treasures of the earth unveiled themselves to him; if too he should have full knowledge of the excellence and usefulness of birds and fishes, of animals, of men, of roots, of trees, of stones, and of waters, write, that not herein is perfect joy." And after a little while he again cried out: "O Brother Leo, although a Brother Minor should know how to preach with such solemnity as to convert all not of the faith to the faith, write, that not herein is perfect joy."

This kind of speaking went on for well-nigh two miles. Then Brother Leo, moved with exceeding marvel, said: "Father, I pray thee, for God's sake, to tell me wherein is perfect joy." To him Saint Francis thus replied: "When we shall come to Saint Mary of the Angels, dripping with rain as we are, and frozen with cold, splashed also with mud, and gnawed with hunger, and we shall knock at the house-door, and the porter

should come angrily and say: 'Who are ye?' and
we should say: 'We are two of your brethren';
and he confronting us should say: 'Nay, ye
are two rogues who are going about everywhere
through the world snatching at the alms of the
poor'; and should not open to us, but should
make us stand in the snow and slush and in
cold and hunger until the night, and then if we
should have borne such insults and repulses
unruffled and unmurmuring, and if we should
think humbly and charitably that both that
porter really knoweth us and that it is God who
moveth his tongue to speak adversely to us,—
then, O Brother Leo, write, that therein is perfect joy. And if we shall have persevered in
knocking, and that porter should come out excited as against troublesome fellows, and should
cruelly cuff us, saying: 'Go hence, ye worthless rascals; get ye to the poor-house. For who
are ye? Ye shall have nothing to eat inside
here!' And if we should bear these things
patiently and receive the insults with hearts full
of love, O Brother Leo, write, that herein is
perfect joy. And if we, distressed on every side,
by pressing hunger, by piercing cold, by the night
creeping on above us, shall knock, and call, and
persist in pleading that the door may be opened
to us, and he then thoroughly roused should say:

'These are shameless fellows and I will make them be quiet!' and coming out with a knotty staff and seizing us by our hoods he fling us to the ground upon the mud and should so beat us with the said staff that everywhere he will cover us with bruises; if such ills, if such insults and stripes we should endure with gladness, thinking that we ought to endure and bear with the utmost patience the sufferings of Christ the Blessed One, then, O Brother Leo, write, that thus there is for us perfect joy.

"Then, O Brother Leo, hearken to the full burthen of this. Amongst all the graces of the Holy Spirit, which Christ hath granted and ever granteth to His friends, is the grace to overcome ourselves, and freely for Christ's sake and for the love of God to bear sufferings, insults, reproaches and want. For in all gifts that excite marvelling we are not able to glory, as they are not ours but God's. For what hast thou that thou hast not received? Yet if thou hast received them, why gloriest thou, as if thou hadst not received them, as if indeed they were thine own alone? But in the cross of tribulation and affliction we are able to glory, for that is ours. Therefore the Apostle saith: 'Be it far from me to glory save in the cross of our Lord Jesus Christ.'"

*   *   *

Once when the holy father Francis, in the
early days of the Order, was staying with Brother
Leo, in a certain little house where they had no
service books, on a certain night, when they rose
up for matins, Saint Francis said to his brother:
"Beloved, we have not a breviary wherewith to
say matins, but that we may spend the time to
the praise of God, as I shall tell thee, so do
thou say, and take thou heed not to change the
words I utter. For thus I shall say: 'O Brother
Francis, thou hast committed so many sins in
the world that thou art deserving of hell.' And
thou, Brother Leo, shalt respond: 'True it is
that thou hast deserved hell.'" Brother Leo,
most guileless, with dove-like simplicity, replied:
"Willingly, father. Begin, in the name of the
Lord." And Saint Francis began to say: "O
Brother Francis, thou hast committed so many
sins in this world that thou art deserving of
hell." And Brother Leo replied: "God will do
by thee so many good deeds that thou wilt go
to Paradise." Then Saint Francis said: "Speak
not thus, Brother Leo, but when I shall say:
'O Brother Francis, thou hast worked so many
iniquitous deeds against God that thou dost deserve
to be accursed,' do thou thus respond: 'Amongst
the accursed thou deservest to be accounted.'"
And Brother Leo said: "Willingly, father."

SAINT FRANCIS

And Saint Francis with many tears and sighs, and smitings of the breast, and in a loud tone, said: "O Lord, God of heaven and earth, so many evil deeds have I wrought against Thee that I deserve to be utterly accursed." And Brother Leo replied: "God will do so unto thee that amongst the blessed thou wilt be singularly blest." And Saint Francis, wondering that he responded quite contrary to that which he had dictated, reprimanding him, said: "Wherefore, Brother Leo, dost thou not respond as I teach thee? By virtue of holy obedience I enjoin thee that according to the words with which I shall instruct thee, thou respond. I shall thus speak: 'O Brother Francis, wretched one, thinkest thou that God will have mercy on thee, when so many sins against Him, the Father of mercies and God of all consolation, thou hast committed, —thinkest thou that thou art worthy to find mercy?' And thou, Brother Leo, little lamb, shalt say: 'In no wise art thou worthy to find mercy.'" And Brother Leo responded thus: "God the Father, whose mercy is greater infinitely than thy sin, will grant thee great mercy, and above all will add unto thee abundant grace."

But Saint Francis, sweetly irate and patiently troubled, said to Brother Leo: "Wherefore,

brother, hast thou against obedience thus pre-
sumed, and now hast so often responded contrary
to what I bade thee?" And then Brother Leo
answered, reverently and with much humility:
"God knoweth, dearest father, that I set before
myself always what thou didst enjoin, but God
made me speak according to His good pleasure
and not according as I had proposed." Marvelling
at which, Saint Francis said to Brother Leo:
"I pray thee, beloved, that this time thou dost
say, when I shall have accused myself as before,
that of mercy I am not worthy." And every
time, these same things he had imposed on
Brother Leo with many tears. Brother Leo
answered: "Say on, father, for this time I will
respond as thou shalt wish." And Saint Francis
exclaimed with tears: "O Francis, wretched one,
thinkest thou that God will have mercy on thee?"
Brother Leo responded: "Yea, father, God will
have mercy on thee. Abundant grace, indeed,
thou shalt receive from God thy Saviour, and He
will exalt thee and glorify thee for ever; for every
one who humbleth himself shall be exalted;—
and I am not able to say otherwise, for it is
God who speaketh through my mouth."

And thus, in this humble contention, with
blinding tears and divine consolation, they kept
vigil until the dawn.

To the praise and glory of our Lord Jesus Christ. Amen.

*   *   *

Once when Saint Francis was grievously ill, Brother Leo tended him with much devotion and affection. When on one occasion Brother Leo stood near the Blessed Francis and gave himself humbly up to prayer, he was rapt in ecstasy and borne away to a great river, swift and wide.

There, as he watched those who were crossing, he saw some of the brethren bearing burdens enter the river. Some at once by the impetuousness of the river were overturned, and the devouring depth closed upon them. Others went as far as a third of the way across the river, and there perished. Others went as far as mid-stream; others almost to the other side; and all, on account of the packages and burdens which they bore, were, in divers ways, according to their various loads, whelmed in the river, and perished cruelly, away from every chance of being rescued. Brother Leo, seeing the great danger, pitied them. Then behold suddenly there appeared some brethren without any burden or package of any kind, and from whom alone poverty shone forth. These entered the river, and passed across without any harm.

But Saint Francis, divining that Brother Leo

68

had seen a vision of some kind, after that Brother
Leo had returned to himself, called him and
said: "Tell me what thou hast seen." And he
told him in due order of what he had seen.
Francis said to him: "True are the things thou
hast seen. The river is the world. The brethren
who are swallowed up by the river are they who
do not really follow their Gospel profession and
remain true to voluntary poverty. But they who
without danger get across are brethren having
the Spirit of God, and who do not love, or desire, or possess, anything earthly, or carnal, but
having food and that with which they are clothed
are therewith content; following Christ in His
nakedness on the Cross, and embracing daily
the burden of His Cross and the yoke of His
obedience—the burden and the yoke most sweet
and light. Wherefore easily and without peril
they pass from things temporal to the things
eternal."

To the praise of our Lord Jesus Christ the
Blessed One.

IX. SAINT FRANCIS AND BROTHER MASSEO.

Saint Francis was dwelling in the House of the Little Portion with Brother Masseo, who in discoursing of God was endowed with grace of utterance and gifted too with great discernment, so that he was greatly loved by the Saint. When on a certain day Saint Francis returned from the wood where he had been praying, and had reached the outlet from the wood, Brother Masseo met him, and wishing to have experience of the extent of the Saint's humility, said to Saint Francis: "Why to thee? Why to thee? Why to thee?" Saint Francis replied: "What saith Brother Masseo?" The brother answered: "All the world seem to come after thee, and all seek to see thee, to listen to thee, and to render obedience to thee. Thou art not comely; thou art not of great knowledge or wisdom; thou art not of noble descent. Whence then is it that all the world should come to thee?"

SAINT FRANCIS AND BROTHER MASSEO

The Blessed Francis, when he heard this, was spiritually exhilarated, and lifting up his face toward heaven, he stood a long while, with his mind steadfastly directed towards God, and then returning to himself, he knelt down, praising and giving thanks to God in great fervour of spirit. Then he turned himself to Brother Masseo; and said : "Wishest thou to know why men come to me ? Wishest thou this to know ? Wishest thou to know and to know well why they come after me ? This cometh to me from the most holy discerning eyes of God, which in every place behold the good and evil. For those blessed and most holy eyes have not seen amongst those who are evil a sinner more vile, more faulty, and more sinful than myself. Since, therefore, He for carrying out this marvellous work upon which He is intent, seeth not upon earth a creature more worthless than I am, He hath for that reason chosen me. For God chooseth the foolish ones of the world to confound the wise, and God chooseth the ignoble and contemptible and weak of the world to confound the noble and the exalted and the strong; that it may be known that the height of virtue is with God and not from the creature; that of all creatures and of all flesh none may glory in His sight; but whosoever glorieth, let him glory in the Lord, that in God alone there may be honour and glory ever discerned."

Then Brother Masseo, at so humble a reply, uttered with such great fervour, was amazed, and knew of a certainty that the holy father was rooted in true humility—was indeed a true and lowly disciple of Christ.

*   *   *

Once Saint Francis was on a road in Tuscany with Brother Masseo, whom by reason of the charm of his words and singular discernment, and on account of the aid which he afforded to himself in his moments of rapture, by answering satisfactorily those whom he met, and by shielding the Saint from view, lest he should be interrupted by any, he most willingly took with him for companion. And when on a certain day they thus walked on together, Brother Masseo was in advance of Saint Francis on the road, by some distance. But when he had come to a certain spot, from which three roads started— for Siena, for Florence, and for Arezzo—said Brother Masseo: "Father, which road ought we to take?" The Saint replied: "That road we will take which God shall wish." To which Brother Masseo answered: "And how shall we be able to know God's will as to this?" The Saint replied: "By the sign which I shall show

thee. Whence, by virtue of holy obedience, I bid
thee that in this parting of the ways, on the spot
forsooth whereon thou hast planted thy feet, thou
turn round and round like boys do, and that thou
do not stop turning round until I shall tell thee
to do so."

But he, as truly obedient, went on so long
turning round there, that by reason of giddiness
brought on by such twirling round, he several
times fell. But as Saint Francis did not stay
him, and he wished to be obedient, he arose and
began again the said twirling round. And when
Brother Masseo had for a long time spun round
quite bravely, Saint Francis said to him: "Stand
firm, and do not move." At once he stopped.
And Saint Francis said: "Towards which road
hast thou thy face looking?" He replied: "Towards Siena." Then said Saint Francis: "That
is the very road along which God wisheth that
we shall go." As they went on, Brother Masseo
marvelled much that Saint Francis had made
him turn round so childishly, in the presence
too of all who were passing by on their everyday
business. Still from a feeling of reverence he
did not dare to say anything to the saintly
father. But when he drew nigh to Siena, and
the people of the city knew of the arrival of
Saint Francis, they came to meet him on the

way, and bore him and his companion aloft, so
that their feet should not touch the ground, until
they reached the bishop's palace.

But in that very hour some of the citizens
were fighting with one another, and already two
had been slain. And Saint Francis arose and
went forth, and preached to the men at variance
with such holy impressiveness that he led them
all back to peace and to great concord. Because
of this work so admirable, the bishop invited
Saint Francis to his palace, and welcomed him
with great honour. But on the morrow, Saint
Francis, truly humble, being one who in his
labours sought nothing except the divine glory,
arose at an early hour with his companion,
and, without a word of farewell to the bishop,
departed.

Whereat Brother Masseo, as he went on,
murmured to himself by the way, and said:
"What is it that this good man hath done?
Yesterday he made me twirl round like a boy,
and to-day to the bishop who hath honoured
him so much he hath neither said a good word,
nor requited him with thanks." And it seemed
to him that all these things had been indiscreet.
At length by a divine impulse returning to himself—to his very heart—and severely censuring
himself, he said: "Brother Masseo, thou art

above measure proud who passest judgment on
deeds of divine import, and thou art deserving
of hell, thou who with thy proud discretion
rebellest against God. For in that way such
holy deeds were wrought by Brother Francis that
if an angel of God had wrought them they could
not have been more wonderful. Wherefore if he
were to enjoin thee to throw stones, even then
thou oughtest to obey him. For all things which
in that way he hath accomplished have proceeded from a divine ordainment, as appeareth
from the best of results that have followed. For
if he had not led back those fighting men to
peace, not only would the sword have slain the
bodies of many—for such slaughter had already
begun—but also, which would have been worse,
the infernal abyss would, with the aid of the
destroyer, have engulfed the souls of many. And
thus it is that thou art foolish and proud, since
thou murmurest at those things which are clearly
in accordance with the Divine will."

Now these things, Brother Masseo, as he
was going on a little distance in front of Saint
Francis, was saying in his heart. But Saint
Francis, enlightened by the Divine Spirit, to
whom all things are made bare and opened out,
called out behind the back of Brother Masseo.
And disclosing the secret thoughts of his heart,

75

he said: "Keep thee to those things which now thou thinkest upon, for they are good and useful to thee, as they are inspired by God. But the first murmuring which thou didst mutter is blind and wicked and proud and sown in thy heart by the devil." Hearing which, Brother Masseo was amazed, as he clearly perceived that Saint Francis knew the hidden secrets of his heart, and above all things that he understood of a certainty that the Spirit of divine grace directed Saint Francis in all his actions.

To the praise and glory of our Lord Jesus Christ. Amen.

*   *   *

Our most Blessed Father Francis wished to humiliate Brother Masseo, so that the manifold gifts which the Most High was bestowing on him might increase from virtue unto virtue. This was when the saintly father was in a certain solitary house with his first companions—of true saintliness—along with whom Brother Masseo was also dwelling. Saint Francis on a certain day, in the presence of all assembled together, said: "O Brother Masseo, these thy brethren have the gift of prayer and contemplation; but thou hast the gift of preaching God's word acceptably to the people who flock to us; and therefore for that reason to the end that they may be the better able to be free to apply themselves to prayer and meditation, I wish that thou shouldst have the care of the gate, of the alms, and of the kitchen. When the brothers eat, thou shalt eat outside the entrance door, so that before ever those who come shall knock at the door, thou shalt satisfy them with some words, and thus it will not behove anyone to go outside except thyself. And this thou shalt do by the merit of holy obedience."

Then Brother Masseo at once, with head inclined and hood drawn back, humbly obeyed, and for many days took charge of the gate, the alms, and the kitchen. But his brethren, as men illuminated by God, began to have inwardly in their hearts much conflict of feeling, as Brother Masseo was a man of great perfection and given to prayer, even as themselves were, and more so, and yet the whole burden of the house was placed upon him. Wherefore they prayed the saintly father that he would deign to distribute the duties among themselves, for in no way were their consciences able to endure that the said brother should be subject to such great fatigues. For besides they felt themselves feeble in their prayers, and in conscience disturbed, while Brother Masseo was not relieved from the said burdens.

The Blessed Francis, listening to their words, assented to their charitable counsels. Calling Brother Masseo, he said: "Brother Masseo, these thy brethren wish to have share in the duties which I have assigned to thee; and therefore I wish that the said duties may be divided amongst them." Humbly and patiently replying, he said: "Father, whatever thou dost assign to me—whether a part or the whole—I deem it wholly assigned by God."

And then Saint Francis, seeing the loving-kindness of the brethren and the lowly meekness of Masseo, preached before them a marvellous discourse on holy humility, teaching them that without that no virtue is acceptable unto God. And after this he divided the duties amongst them, and with the grace of the Holy Spirit, blessed them all.

To the praise of God.

*   *   *

The wondrous servant of God and true disciple of Christ, Saint Francis, desired that in all things he might conform himself to Christ. As Christ sent His disciples by twos into every city and place unto which He Himself had the intention to go, so Saint Francis after he had gathered around him companions to the number of twelve, dispersed them two and two to preach throughout the world. And that he might show to others in himself an example of true obedience, he himself first, in imitation of Christ the Blessed One, began to do as well as to teach. Wherefore having sent his companions through various parts of the world, he himself having chosen Brother Masseo as his companion began to journey on the road towards France.

When they had arrived at certain habitations, their bodily frames being distressed by hunger, they must needs, as their rule bade them, beg for bread. So Saint Francis went by one street and Brother Masseo by another. But Saint Francis was a man lowly in aspect and small in stature, and thus was looked down upon as a poor little wretch by those who knew him not, and received only a few morsels of stale bread and little scraps. But to Brother Masseo, since he was comely and tall in person, were given plenty of good pieces and new bread without stint.

But when they met together in a certain spot, they there found a spring and at its margin a fine broad stone, at which they much rejoiced. They placed upon that stone the fragments of bread which they had begged. When Saint Francis saw that the pieces of bread of Brother Masseo were more in number and better in quality than his own, he rejoiced in spirit with the joy of poverty, and said: "O Brother Masseo, we are not worthy of such great treasure." And this he repeated many times, gradually raising his voice. Brother Masseo replied: "Father most dear, how can we talk of treasure where there is such great penury, for there is not here cloth, or knife, or plate, or bowl, or house, or table, or waiting-man, or waiting-maid?" Saint Francis answered: "And this I deem a great treasure, that there are none of those things which human industry provideth. But whatsoever else is here is altogether set before us by Divine providence, as clearly appeareth in the bread we have begged, in the stone so beautiful, in the spring so sparkling. Wherefore I wish that we pray to God that the treasure of holy poverty, so noble, which hath Himself as its provider, we may love with all our heart."

And from these morsels of bread, and from the spring—from the food and drink partaken of gladly with hymns of divine praise, they rose up that they might push on towards France. When they came to a certain church they went inside, and Saint Francis hid himself behind the altar, to pray. And there he received from a divine vision such excessive fervour, altogether setting on fire his soul with the yearning love of holy poverty, that it seemed as though from face and lips there shone forth and were breathed forth the glow of heavenly love.

And coming out to his companion, with thus the enkindled fire blazing forth, he said: "Ah! Ah! Ah! Brother Masseo, give thyself to me!" And this he said thrice. Brother Masseo, marvelling at the fervour so vehement, when for the third time Saint Francis said: "Give thyself to me!" cast himself entirely beneath the arms of the holy father. Then Saint Francis, with openmouthed exultation, and with the fervour of the Spirit, and with a strong resounding utterance "Ah! Ah! Ah!" raised Brother Masseo with his breath into the air, and forced him before him as far as might be the length of a long lance. Seeing which Brother Masseo was amazed greatly at such marvellous fervour of the Holy Spirit. And he related afterwards to his companions that in that impulsive action of Saint Francis he felt such great sweetness and consolation of the Holy Spirit that never in his life did he remember to have had so mighty a solace.

Afterwards Saint Francis said to Brother Masseo: "Beloved companion, let us go to Rome to Saint Peter and Saint Paul, and entreat them to teach us and help us to possess the unspeakable treasure of most holy poverty." And Saint Francis further said: "My very dear and much loved brother, the treasure of beatific poverty is so full of honour and so divine that we are not worthy to store it up in our vessels of such lowliness; since poverty is that celestial virtue by which all things earthly and transitory are trodden on, by which all obstacles are removed from amongst us, so that the human soul may be freely joined to the Lord God Eternal. This it is which enableth the soul still placed on earth to converse with angels in heaven. This it is, that was associated with Christ on the Cross; that was hidden with Christ in the tomb; that rose with Christ and ascended into heaven; for even in this life it granteth to souls that love it the gift of alertness of flight towards heaven, since it alone guardeth the arms of humility and love. To this end let us entreat the most holy apostles of Christ that they who were lovers of this evangelical pearl may obtain for us this grace from the Lord Jesus Christ, that He, who was observer and teacher of holy poverty, may deign, by His most holy mercy, to grant unto us that we may be worthy to be true devotees and humble disciples of most precious and most lovable evangelical poverty."

So when they arrived at Rome they entered the church of Saint Peter. And Saint Francis betook himself to one corner of the church, and

Brother Masseo to another, to beseech God and
His holy apostles to instruct them and aid them
so that they might become possessed of the
treasure of holy poverty. These things they asked
for with great devotion and with many tears.
But whilst they were so humbly persevering in
prayer, lo! Blessed Peter and Blessed Paul
appeared amid great brightness to Saint Francis,
embracing him with affection, and saying:
"Brother Francis, because thou seekest and
longest for that which Christ Himself and His
holy apostles were devoted to, therefore we make
known to thee on the part of the Lord Jesus Christ
that thy desire is fulfilled. And the Lord Jesus
Christ hath sent us to thee to announce to thee
that thy prayer is heard, and that the treasure of
most holy poverty is granted to thee and to those
who follow thee. And to thee on the part of
Christ we say that whosoever shall perfectly
follow this desire by thy example, may be assured
of the kingdom of blessedness. And blessed of
the Lord shalt thou be and all who follow thee."

With these words they withdrew, leaving him
inwardly consoled. But Saint Francis, rising up
from prayer, went to his companion, and asked
of him if any bestowal had been made to him
from God. He replied that nothing had been
vouchsafed to him. Then Saint Francis told how

the holy apostles had appeared to himself, and the words from on high they had revealed to him. With which they both were filled with such joy and gladness, that they let slip the intention to go to France which they had at first adopted, and returned with haste to the Valley of Spoleto where this celestial and angelic way of life had to be entered upon.

        *   *   *

The holy companions of our Blessed Father Francis, poor indeed in the things of this world, but rich towards God, did not seek to become rich in gold or silver, but most eagerly strove to be enriched with the holy virtues by which advance is made to true and eternal exaltation. Wherefore it happened one day that as Brother Masseo, one of the chosen brethren of the holy father, and his companions were talking of God, one of them said that there was a certain friend of God who possessed great grace both for the life of action and for the life of contemplation. With this he had a profound depth of humility, by reason of which he thought himself the greatest sinner, which humility sanctified him and strengthened him and caused him to continually increase in the aforesaid gifts, and, what is better, never permitted him to fall away from God.

As Brother Masseo heard of these marvellous

84

things and perceived that humility was the treasure
of the eternal life of salvation, to such an extent
did he burn with desire to possess that virtue of
humility, most worthy of the embrace of God,
that in great fervour, raising his countenance
towards heaven, he bound himself most firmly by
a vow never to wish to be joyful in this world
until he felt that humility in the fulness of its
brightness was present in his soul. And after
making this vow with this sacred intention, he
remained almost continually shut up in his cell,
and while he was so secluded, he unceasingly
afflicted himself with sighings before God that
cannot be uttered; for it seemed to him that he
was a man entirely deserving of hell, unless he
arrived at that most holy humility by which that
friend of God, of whom he had heard, thought
himself, though full of virtues, less worthy than
all others, yea indeed deemed himself as utterly
meriting hell.

While thus in sadness, Brother Masseo remained during very many days, sacrificing himself
in hunger and thirst and many tears. It chanced
that on a certain day he entered into the wood,
and as he went through it, because of the aforesaid
vehement desire, he uttered laments, cries, and
tearful sighings, entreating that the virtue he
desired should be given to him.

And because God brings restoration to the contrite in heart, and hearkens to the voices of the humble, a voice was heard by him from heaven, crying twice: "Brother Masseo! Brother Masseo!" He by the Holy Spirit made conscious whence the voice sounded to him, said: "My Lord!" And the Lord said to him: "What wouldst thou give, what wouldst thou give, to possess this grace?" And Brother Masseo replied: "The eyes out of my head." And the Lord said to him: "And I will that thou shalt have the grace and thine eyes too." Brother Masseo was so filled with the grace of the desired humility, and with the light of God, that continually he was in joy. And often when he prayed he would break forth into a harmonious strain of joy, or with a subdued voice uttered like a dove, "Oo, Oo, Oo," and with cheerful face gave himself up to joyful meditation, and henceforth became most humble. He indeed reached the greatest humility, and amongst men accounted himself the least of all.

Brother James of Fallerone, of sacred memory, asked him wherefore he did not vary his note in his joy. He replied with great gladness: "Since in one thing is found every good, it is not needful that the note should vary."

To the praise of our Lord Jesus Christ. Amen.

X. SAINT FRANCIS AND THE ROBBERS.

To a certain hermitage of the brethren above Borgo San Sepolcro there came once on a time for bread robbers who used to lurk in the woods and despoil men who were travelling through them. Certain brethren were wont to say that it was not a good thing to give them alms, but others out of compassion would give with the thought of moving them to penitence.

In the meanwhile the Blessed Francis came to that place, and the brethren asked him whether it were a good thing to give them alms, and the Blessed Francis said to them: "If ye will do as I shall tell you I trust in the Lord that ye shall win their souls. Go ye therefore and procure food, bread and good wine, and carry the same to them in the wood where they dwell, and cry out saying: 'Brother robbers, come to us, for we are brethren and are bringing you good bread and good wine!'

"They will come at once. Then do ye spread a napkin on the ground, and upon it place the bread and the wine and serve the same humbly and cheerfully until they shall have eaten. But after the meal do ye talk to them of the Word of God, and do ye put to them at last for the love of God this first petition that forsooth they promise you that they will not murder or do harm to the person of anyone. For if ye shall ask everything at once they will not listen to you; but such they will at once promise you because of your humility and charity.

"Now on another day, on account of their good promise carry unto them with the bread and wine eggs and cheese and serve them until they shall have eaten. And after the meal ye shall say to them: 'Why do ye stay here the whole day to die of hunger, and endure so many hardships and with this commit so many wrongs by will and deed for which ye are destroying your own souls unless ye be converted to the Lord? Better it is that ye serve the Lord, and He in this world will give unto you the things needful for your bodies and at last will save your souls.' Then the Lord will inspire them so that because of your humility and patience which ye shall have shown unto them they will be converted."

And so the brethren did everything as the Blessed Francis had said to them, and the robbers themselves by the grace and mercy of God did listen to them and did observe from letter to letter and from point to point everything whatsoever the brethren had humbly sought from them. Yea, because of the humility and familiarity of the brethren towards them they began also to serve the brethren humbly, carrying on their shoulders logs up to the hermitage, and at last some of them entered the Religion. But others confessing their sins did penance for those they had committed, promising as they clasped the hands of the brethren that they would in the days to come be willing to live by the labour of their hands and never again to do the same misdeeds as before.

XI. SAINT FRANCIS AND
JOHN THE SAINT.

Saint Francis went to a certain church in a
village subject to the city of Assisi, and began to
sweep out the same in a humble way and to clean
it, and straightway there went a rumour of him
throughout the whole village, for he was seen
gladly and was more gladly listened to by the
people thereabout. But when a certain rustic of
wonderful simplicity who was ploughing in his
field, John by name, heard of this, he at once
went to him and found him sweeping out the
church humbly and with devotion. And he said
to him: "Brother, give me the broom, as I wish
to help thee." And receiving the broom from his
hands, he swept that which was left.

And as they were sitting together he said to
the Blessed Francis: "Brother, a long time ago I
had the desire to serve God, and especially after
I heard the report about thee and thy brethren;
but I knew not how I might come unto thee.
Now therefore after that it hath pleased the Lord
that I should see thee I wish to do whatsoever
shall please thee."

The Blessed Francis taking note of his fervour
rejoiced in the Lord greatly, since at that time he

had few brethren, and it seemed to him that on
account of his simplicity and purity the rustic
ought to be a good Religious. He however said
to him: "Brother, if thou wishest to be of our life
and society, it behoveth thee to deprive thyself of
all that is thine—of all that without offence thou
canst lay claim to,—and give to the poor according to the counsel of the Holy Gospel, inasmuch
as all my brothers who were able have done the
same."

When he heard this he at once went to the
field where he had left his oxen, and unloosed
them and led one of them into the presence of the
Blessed Francis, and said to him: "Brother, for
so many years have I served my father and all of
my house, and although this is but a small part of
mine inheritance, I am willing to receive this ox
for my share and to give it to the poor as it shall
seem best to thee." But when his kinsfolk and
his brothers who were still very young saw that he
wished to leave them, they began—all of the
household—to weep so pitifully and to lament
with such sorrowful voices, that the Blessed
Francis was moved thereby with compassion,
because the family was large and needing help.
And the Blessed Francis said to them: "Get
ready some food for all of us and let us all eat of
it with one another, and do not lament, for I will

91

make you very glad." Now they straightway got ready and they all had food together with great cheerfulness.

Now after the meal the Blessed Francis said: "This your son is willing to serve God and on this account ye ought not to be sad but greatly to rejoice. For unto you not only in the sight of God but also in the esteem of this world is it accounted as a great honour and advantage of souls and bodies that God should be honoured by one of your flesh and that all our brethren shall become your sons and brothers. And because he is a creature of God and wisheth to serve his Creator, whom to serve is indeed to reign, I am not able and I ought not to restore him to you, but that concerning him ye may have consolation, it is my wish that he shall bestow upon you as upon those who are poor this ox which is his own, although according to the Gospel he ought to give it unto others who are poor." And they were all comforted by the words of Saint Francis and were greatly rejoiced because of the ox which was returned to them and because they were indeed very poor.

And because pure and holy simplicity was only too pleasing to the Blessed Francis, whether it was in himself or in others, he forthwith clothed John in the habit of the Religion and led him away humbly as his companion. For he was of such simplicity that he believed that he was bound to do in all things as the Blessed Francis did.

Wherefore when the Blessed Francis would stay in any church or in any place to pray, he also would watch him so that to all his actions and gestures he might entirely conform himself. So that if the Blessed Francis did bend his knees or raise his hands towards heaven, or spat or sighed, he also did all in like manner. But when the Blessed Francis had pondered on this he began, with great pleasantry, to chide him for this sort of simplicity. To whom he answered: "Brother, I promised to do all things that thou doest, and therefore I must copy thee in everything."

And at this the Blessed Francis marvelled and rejoiced marvellously, seeing that he was of such purity and simplicity.

But he afterwards began to advance to such excellence that the Blessed Francis and the other brethren did all very greatly marvel at his perfection. After some little time he died, having attained to exceeding holiness. Wherefore afterwards the Blessed Francis, with much gladness of mind and body, would amongst the brethren tell of his conversation, calling him not Brother John, but John the Saint.

XII. SAINT FRANCIS AND
CARDINAL UGOLINO.

The Lord Bishop of Ostia, who was afterwards
Pope Gregory, when he came to the chapter of
the brethren at Saint Mary of the Little Portion,
in order to see the dormitory of the brethren,
entered their house, with many knights and clergy.
When he saw that the brethren lay on the ground
and had nothing beneath them save a little straw
and some cushions all tattered, with no pillows for
their heads, he began to weep aloud before them
all, and to say : "Look, here it is that the brethren
sleep, while we wretched ones use so many super-
fluities! How will it be with us?" Whereupon
he and all the others were much edified. Further-
more he saw there no table, as the brethren did
eat on the ground in that house.

*   *   *

Once when the Blessed Francis was on a visit
to the Lord Bishop of Ostia, who was afterwards
Pope Gregory, near the hour of meal-time, he
went in a stealthy sort of way from door to door

for alms. When he returned, the Lord Bishop of
Ostia had gone in to sit at table, with many
knights and nobles. Now the Blessed Francis
drew nigh and placed upon the table in the
presence of the Cardinal the alms which he had
received, and took a place at the table next to the
Cardinal, who wished that the Blessed Francis
should always sit next to him. The Cardinal was
then a little ashamed because the Blessed Francis
had gone for alms and had placed them upon the
table; but he said nothing to him then, because of
those who were sitting at the table. And when
the Blessed Francis had eaten a little he took of
his alms and sent a little to each knight and to
each of the chaplains of the Lord Cardinal, in the
name of the Lord God. These all received the
same with great gladness and devotion, spreading
out their hoods and scarves, and some did eat
thereof, and some did place the food aside out of
devotion to the Blessed Francis. Now the Lord
Bishop of Ostia rejoiced greatly at their devotion,
especially because those alms were not of bread
from wheat.

After the meal the Lord Cardinal entered into
his chamber, leading with him the Blessed Francis.
There raising his arms he embraced the Blessed
Francis with very great joy and exultation, saying
to him: "Wherefore, my most simple brother,

hast thou done me to-day this shame as to come to my house, which is the house of thy brethren, and go forth from it for alms?"

To him the Blessed Francis replied: "O my Lord, I have indeed shown thee greatest honour, because when a retainer doeth his duty and fulfilleth his obedience to his lord, he doeth honour to his lord; and it behoveth me to be a pattern and example for your poor men, chiefly because I know that in this Religion of the Brethren, there are and will be Brothers Minor in name and in deed, who, on account of the love of God and by the unction of the Holy Spirit who will teach them in all things, will humble themselves to every humility and subjection and service of their brethren. Some also there will be of them who, kept back by shame, or by reason of evil custom, disdain and will disdain to humble themselves and behave themselves lowlily by going forth to seek alms and doing other servile acts, by reason of which it behoveth me by deed to teach them who are and shall be in religion that in this world and in the future they may be inexcusable before God. When therefore I am staying with you who are our Lord and will be our Pope, and with other magnates and rich men of this world, who for love of the Lord God, with much devotion not only receive me into your houses, but even compel

me to come to you, I will not be ashamed to go
forth for alms, indeed I wish to have and to hold
this as in the sight of God of the greatest nobility
and royal dignity, and as being in honour of Him
who when He was Lord of all, was yet willing to
become for us the servant of all, and when He
was rich and glorious in His majesty came as One
poor and despised in our humility. Wherefore I
wish that the brethren—they that are now such,
and they that shall be in time to come—should
know that a greater consolation of soul and body
I have when I sit at the very poor table of the
brethren, and see before me poor scraps of alms
which are got from door to door for the love of the
Lord God, than when I sit at your table and at the
tables of other lords, abundantly set out with
divers dishes. For the bread of alms is holy
bread which the praise and love of the Lord God
sanctifieth, so that when a brother goeth forth for
alms he ought first to say : 'Praised and blessed
be the Lord God.' Afterwards he ought to say:
'Give us alms for the love of the Lord God.'"

And by the utterance of such words as these
by the Blessed Francis the Cardinal was greatly
edified, and said to him : "My son, what is good in
thine eyes, that do, since God is with thee and thou
art with Him."

For such was the will of the Blessed Francis,

and many times he said it, that a brother ought
not to hesitate about going forth for alms, on
account of the great merit thereof, and lest he
should be ashamed to go forth afterwards. Yea,
indeed, by so much the more noble and superior
in the world was a brother the more was he
gladdened and edified concerning him, when he
went forth for alms and did other servile work
such as the brethren then did.

* * *

In the city of Rome, when those two bright
luminaries of the world, forsooth the Blessed
Francis and the Blessed Dominic, were together
in the presence of the Lord Bishop of Ostia, who
afterwards was Pope, and by turns gave utterance
to words flowing forth like honey as they dis-
coursed about God, to them at last spoke the
Lord Bishop: "In the primitive Church bishops
and prelates were poor, and were men fervent in
charity and not in worldly desires. Why therefore
do we not make of your brothers, bishops and
prelates who would prevail over all others as
patterns and examples?"

Then sprang up between the Saints a humble
and devout dispute as to who should first venture
upon a reply—a dispute rather, not as to which of
the two should take the lead, but as to which
should hold back. But at length the humility of

Francis gained this, that he should not first reply, and he gained this over Dominic, that he by first replying should humbly be obedient.

Therefore the Blessed Dominic said, as he made answer: "My Lord, unto good degree have my brethren been uplifted if they would only know it; and so far as it is possible for me I shall never consent that they advance to any height of dignity."

Then the Blessed Francis, bending himself before the said Lord Cardinal, said: "My Lord, Minors are my brethren called, to the end that they may not presume to be made Brothers Major. Their calling teacheth them to dwell on one level, and to tread in the footsteps of the humility of Christ, so that thus they may at last be exalted more than others, with respect to the Saints. For if thou dost wish that they should bring forth fruit in the Church of God retain them and preserve them in the state accordant with their vocation, and if they should climb up towards high positions cast them back violently to their own level, and to any prelacy never permit them to ascend."

These were the replies of the holy men, and at the close of the replies of both, the Lord Bishop was much edified and gave abundant thanks to God.

Now as both were departing together, the Blessed Dominic besought the Blessed Francis that he would deign to give him the cord with which he was cinctured. The Blessed Francis refused out of humility, just as Dominic had asked for it out of charity. At length the happy devotion of the asker prevailed, and the cord of the Blessed Francis that the Blessed Dominic received through the urgency of his love, was girded beneath his tunic, and henceforward devoutly worn.

At last the one did place his hands between the hands of the other, and each commended himself to the other in the sweetness of mutual salutation. And Saint Dominic said to Saint Francis: "I would wish, Brother Francis, one Religion to be made, thine and mine, and both to live in the Church on the same foundation." When they finally separated themselves from each other, the Blessed Dominic said to many who were standing by: "Of a truth I tell you that all the Religious ought to imitate this holy man Francis, so great is the perfection of his sanctity."

*　　　*　　　*

At the close of the chapter at which many brethren were sent to certain provinces beyond the sea, the Blessed Francis remained with some of the brethren, and said to them: "Dearest brethren, it behoveth me to be the pattern and example of all the brethren. If therefore I have sent brethren to distant parts to endure toils and shame, hunger and thirst, and other hardships, it is just, and holy humility requireth, that I in like manner should go to some far-distant province, so that the brothers may the more patiently endure adversities when they shall have heard that I endure the same. Go therefore and pray to the Lord, that He may enable me to choose that province which may be the more to His praise and the advantage of souls and a good ensample of our Religion."

For it was the custom of the most holy father, when he desired to go to some province, to pray first to the Lord, and to send brethren to pray that the Lord would direct his heart to go thither where it was the most pleasing unto Him.

The brethren therefore went to pray, and when they had ended their praying they returned to him. And at once he spoke to them with joy: "In the name of our Lord Jesus Christ and of the glorious Virgin Mary, His Mother, and of all the Saints, I choose the province of France, wherein is a Catholic people, chiefly because amongst other Catholics they show great reverence towards the Body of Christ, which is greatly pleasing unto me, and accordingly with them I will most willingly have converse."

The Blessed Francis chose such of the brethren as he wished to take with him, and said to them: "In the name of the Lord, go ye two and two by the way humbly and reverently, and especially with strict silence from dawn until after tierce, praying unto the Lord in your hearts and not giving utterance amongst you to idle and useless words. For although ye should be walking along, yet your converse should be as subdued and reverent as if ye were in a hermitage or in a cell. For wheresoever we are and are walking we have always with us our cell. For Brother Body is our cell, and the soul is the hermit who dwelleth within the cell to pray unto the Lord and to meditate upon Him. Wherefore if the soul will not remain in quietness in her cell, of little advantage for the Religious is the cell made by hand."

And when he had arrived at Florence, he found there the Lord Ugolino, the Bishop of Ostia, who afterwards was Pope Gregory. He, when he had heard from the Blessed Francis that he wished to go to France, forbade him to go there, saying: "Brother, I do not wish that you should go beyond the mountains, because there are many prelates in the Roman Court who would gladly hinder the good work of the Religion. Yet I and the other Cardinals who love the Religion will protect it gladly and will aid the same, if thou wilt remain within the bounds of this province."

And to him the Blessed Francis said: "My Lord, there will be great shame for me, when I shall have sent other brethren of mine to far-distant provinces, if I shall remain in these provinces, and shall not be a partaker of the tribulations which they will suffer for the Lord's sake."

But to him spoke the bishop as if upbraiding him: "Why hast thou sent thy brethren so far away to die of hunger and to endure other tribulations?"

To him replied the Blessed Francis, speaking with great fervour and in the spirit of prophecy: "My Lord, do you think that the Lord hath sent the brethren for the sake of these provinces only? But I tell you in truth that God hath chosen and hath sent the brethren for the benefit and salvation of the souls of all men of this world. Not only in lands of the faithful but also in lands of the infidel shall they be received and shall they win many souls."

And the Lord Bishop of Ostia marvelled at his words, affirming that he spoke the truth.

Still even so he did not permit him to go to
France ; but the Blessed Francis sent thither
Brother Pacifico with many other brethren. He
himself however returned to the Vale of Spoleto.

*   *   *

The Blessed Francis once went to Rome, that
he might stay with the Lord Bishop of Ostia, and
when he had stayed there some days with him he
visited also the Lord Cardinal Leo, who was very
devoted to the Blessed Francis. And because it
was then winter-time and altogether unfit for
walking by reason of the cold and the wind and
the rain, the Cardinal begged him to remain
some days with him and take his food from him
as one of the poor along with the other poor who
fed daily in his house.

Now this he said because he knew that the
Blessed Francis always wished to be received as
a poor man wheresoever he was entertained, even
though the Lord Pope and the Cardinals were to
receive him with the greatest devotion and
reverence, and to venerate him as a Saint. And
he added : "I will give thee a good retired dwelling-
room where thou wilt be able to pray and eat as
thou wishest."

Then Brother Angelo Tancredi, who was one
of the twelve first brothers, who also was staying
with the said Cardinal, said to the Blessed

Francis: "Brother, there is close by here a certain tower, very spacious and retired, where thou wilt be able to remain as if in a hermitage." This tower, when the Blessed Francis saw it, pleased him, and having returned to the Lord Cardinal, he said to him: "My Lord, perchance I will stay with you for some days."

And the Lord Cardinal rejoiced greatly. Therefore Brother Angelo went and prepared in the tower a room for the Blessed Francis and his companion. And because the Blessed Francis was unwilling to descend thence so long as he remained with the Cardinal, and was not willing for any one to come to him, Brother Angelo promised and arranged to carry there food daily for him and his companion.

And when the Blessed Francis went there with his companion the first night, he said that his sleep was disturbed by demons, whom he thought to be sent by the Lord, as His appointed servants to correct and chastise those whom He loved. And so by these messengers of the Lord the Blessed Francis was buffeted and chastised for having unwittingly offended.

And said he: "It may be that the Lord hath chastised me because although the Lord Cardinal doth gladly show kindness unto me, and that it is necessary for my body to receive this refreshment,

my brothers who are going through the world
enduring hunger and many tribulations, and other
brethren who abide in hermitages and poor little
houses, when they shall hear that I am staying
with the Lord Cardinal, will have occasion to murmur against me, saying, 'We are enduring so many
hardships, and he himself has his consolations.'

"For I have ever to give them a good example,
since for this I am given to them : for the brethren
are more edified when I remain in poor little
houses amongst them than in others, and they
bear more patiently their tribulations when they
hear that I also bear the same."

And so this was the great and continual desire
of our father, that in all things he should offer
a good example, and from the other brethren
remove occasion of murmuring about himself.
And by reason of this, both when well and when
ill, so often and so much did he suffer, that whoever of the brethren knew this as we who were
with him until the day of his death, as often as
they read of him so suffering, or bring his sufferings back to their memory, are not able to keep
themselves from tears, and would themselves
undergo all tribulations and distresses with greater
patience and joy.

The Blessed Francis therefore came down in
the early morning from the top of the tower, and

went to the Lord Cardinal, to tell of all things that had happened to him, and what he with his companion had endured. Indeed he even said to the Cardinal: "Men think that I am a saintly man, and lo! demons have driven me forth from my retreat."

And the Lord Cardinal rejoiced very much with him. It is true that he knew and venerated him as a Saint, yet he would not gainsay him when he no longer wished to remain there.

And so the Blessed Francis, uttering a farewell, returned to the hermitage of Fonte Columbano near Rieti.

* * *

When the Blessed Francis was in the Chapter General at Saint Mary of the Little Portion, —called the Chapter of the Wattles, because there were not any dwellings there except such as were made of wattles, and where there were present five thousand brethren,—very many of them who were wise and learned went to the Lord Bishop of Ostia who was there, and said to him: "My Lord, we wish that you should persuade the Blessed Francis that he follow the counsel of the brethren that are wise, and permit himself some-times to be guided by them." And they called attention to the Rule of S. Benedict, to that of S. Augustine, and to that of S. Bernard; all

teaching such and such things as to those who
live in their Orders.

When the Cardinal had recited all these things
to the Blessed Francis, as though by way of
admonition, the Blessed Francis, returning no
answer to him, took him by the hand and led him
to the brethren gathered together in chapter, and
thus spoke to the brethren in the fervour and
valour of the Holy Spirit : " My brothers ! my
brothers ! the Lord hath called me by the way
of simplicity and of humility, and this way hath
He in truth pointed out to me for myself and
for those who are willing to trust in me and to
follow me. And therefore I wish that ye do not
name to me any Rule, either that of S. Benedict, or
that of S. Augustine, or that of S. Bernard, or any
way and method of living except that which hath
been mercifully made known and imparted unto
me by the Lord. And the Lord hath told me that
He wished me to be a new covenant in this world
and desired not to lead us by any other way than
by the knowledge of that. But by means of your
knowledge and your wisdom God will confound you, and I trust in the servants of the Lord
who carry out His decrees, that by them God
will punish you, and that ye will yet return to
your right attitude, whether with your fault-
finding ye will or will not."

Then the Cardinal was exceedingly amazed, and gave no reply, and all the brethren feared very much.

*   *   *

So great was the fervour of love and compassion of the Blessed Francis towards the sorrows and sufferings of Christ, and to such a degree also did he afflict himself daily both inwardly and outwardly, in contemplation of the Passion itself, that he had no care for his own infirmities. Wherefore since for a long time up to the day of his death he had suffered from weakness of the stomach and liver and spleen, and from the time that he returned from beyond the sea he had continuously the greatest trouble with his eyes, he was nevertheless unwilling to take any trouble about getting himself cured.

Wherefore the Lord Bishop of Ostia, seeing that he was and ever had been thus austere towards his own body, and especially because he had already begun to lose the sight of his eyes, and because he was unwilling to have himself made well, spoke to him words of admonition with great pity and compassion : " Brother, thou dost not well in not trying to be cured, since thy life and health are greatly useful to the brethren and to the laity and to the whole Church. For if thou hast compassion on thy brethren who are ill, and ever hast been to them pitiful and merciful, in such great need of thine own thou oughtest not to be cruel to thyself. Wherefore I command thee that thou cause thyself to be healed and succoured."

For the most holy father was wont to take what was bitter for sweet, since he derived continually unbounded sweetness from the lowliness and the footsteps of the Son of God.

*   *   *

When Saint Francis was severely suffering in his eyes, the Lord Cardinal Ugolino, the protector of the Order, who loved him deeply, gave him this command that he should go to Rieti, where were the best of physicians for the eyes. Now the Blessed Francis, having received the letter of the Lord Cardinal, went first to San Damiano where was Saint Clara, the most devout spouse of Christ. For he had proposed, before he should take his departure, to visit her and console her, and afterwards to proceed to Rieti.

But when he had gone to San Damiano, on the first night following, he was so seriously ailing in his eyes that he was not able to see the light. Wherefore he not being able to go on with his journey, the Blessed Clara caused to be made for him a little cell of wattles and reeds, in which Saint Francis might dwell and obtain greater repose. And he remained there fifty days, in such great pain from his eyes, and from annoyance caused by a multitude of mice, that he was not able to rest either by day or by night. Then the Blessed Francis recognising this to be a scourge from God, began to give God thanks, and to praise Him with his whole heart and mouth, and from the very recesses of his soul to cry out that he was deserving of his illness and perplexities and that he merited much greater troubles. And with this he prayed to the Lord, saying: " O Lord Jesus Christ, the good Shepherd, who for us unworthy ones underwent severe hardships, grant to me thy little sheep grace and valour, that in the midst of no tribulation, or perplexity, or sorrow, I may draw back from Thee."

And when he had uttered this prayer, a voice came to him from heaven, saying: " Francis, tell me : If all the earth were gold, and the sea and rivers and springs were balsam, and all mountains and hills and rocks were of precious stones, and thou shouldst find another treasure more noble than them all, as much more noble as gold is than earth, and as balsam is than water, and as precious stones are than mountains and rocks, and if to thee were given instead of thine illness that treasure so dear, wouldst thou not rejoice much ? " Saint Francis replied : " Lord, I am not worthy of so precious a treasure." Then said the Lord to him : " Rejoice now, Brother Francis, because it is the treasure of eternal life which on thee I have bestowed, and from this time I entrust it with thee, and this illness and affliction of thine is the earnest of that blessed treasure."

Then the Blessed Francis, made very joyful, called his companions, and said : " Let us go to Rieti, to the Lord Cardinal." And consoling the Blessed Clara with words divine and flowing like honey, and making a humble farewell to her, as was his wont, he took the road towards Rieti.

When he drew nigh to Rieti so great a multitude of people followed him that on this account he refrained from entering the city, but turned aside to a certain church distant from Rieti about two miles.

XIII. SAINT FRANCIS AT RIETI.

When he had preached to the people in Rieti
in the piazza of the city, at the close of his sermon
there rose up at once the bishop of the same city,
a man in every way discreet and spiritual. He
said to the people : " The Lord from the beginning
since He planted and builded His Church, hath
ever enlightened her by means of holy men, who
by word and example, would help on her perfection ; but now in this latest hour He hath
enlightened her with this poor little despised and
unlettered man, Francis. On account of this
ye are constrained to love and honour the Lord
and to keep yourselves from sins, for not thus
doeth He with every nation."

Having finished these words the bishop came
down from the place where he had preached and
went to the Cathedral Church. Drawing nigh to
him, the Blessed Francis bowed to him and threw
himself at his feet, and said : " In truth I tell
you, my Lord Bishop, that no man hath done
me so much honour in this world as you have
done to-day ; for other men say : ' This is a holy

man !' attributing glory and sanctity to me and
not to the Creator; but you, as one who is discerning, have separated the precious from the
unworthy."

For when the Blessed Francis was praised,
and spoken of as a Saint, he would reply to such
words, saying : " I am not yet assured that I may
not fail in what I strive for and have sons and
daughters, for in whatsoever hour the Lord shall
take away from me the treasure which unto me
He hath commended, what else would remain
with me but body and soul such as even infidels
have? Indeed I ought to believe that if the Lord
had conferred upon a robber or an infidel as
many excellent gifts as on myself, even they
would be more faithful than I. For as in a
picture of the Lord and the Blessed Virgin
painted on wood, the wood and the paint attribute
nothing to themselves, so the servant of God is a
kind of picture of God in which God is honoured
on account of His excellent gifts conferred; but
he himself to himself ought to attribute nothing,
since in respect of God he is less than wood and
paint; he is indeed pure nothing. And therefore to God alone glory and honour must be
rendered, but to himself only shame and tribulation, whilst he liveth amid the miseries of this
world."

XIV. SAINT FRANCIS AT RIVO TORTO.

The Blessed Francis, wandering round through cities and castles, began in each place to preach more perfectly and with increasing fulness, not in the beguiling words of human wisdom, but in the teaching and truth and valour of the Holy Spirit, heralding boldly the Kingdom of God. For he was a truth-proclaiming preacher, strengthened by apostolic authority, using no flatteries, refusing to employ wordy blandishments; since whatsoever he persuaded others to by speech, that he had first persuaded himself to show forth by deed, so that he might speak out the truth most faithfully.

They who listened to him marvelled at the force of his discourses, and at their truth which man had not made known unto him. Even the lettered and the learned, and very many of them, hastened to see and hear him, as a man of another world. From that time many nobles and those of low estate, clergy and laymen, borne on by the breath of a divine inspiration, began to follow closely the footsteps of the Blessed Francis, and throwing from them worldly cares and display, gave themselves up to living under his discipline.

Thus far the blessed father was dwelling in holy converse with others in a certain place near Assisi, which is called Rivo Torto, Winding Stream, where was a certain deserted hut, so inconveniently small, that they were scarcely able to sit down or seek repose in it. There very often in their want of bread they would eat beetroot which in their distress they would beg for here and there. The man of God wrote the names of the brethren upon the beams of this hut, so that whoever wished to rest, or to pray, might know his own place, lest through the narrowness or the inconvenience of the hut, any unwelcome noise should disturb the silence of the mind.

But on a certain day, while the brethren were dwelling in this hut, it happened that a rustic came there with his ass, seeking shelter there for the ass and himself; and lest he should have admission refused by the brethren he hastened in with the ass, saying to the same: " Get well in, for we shall do well in this place." The holy father hearing this and being made aware of the

rustic's intention, was greatly troubled in spirit ;
for the rustic made a great noise with his ass,
disturbing all the brethren, who were then preparing themselves for silence and prayer. Therefore the man of God said to the brethren : " I
know, brethren, that God hath not called us to
provide shelter for an ass, or to abide in a place
frequented by men, but that we should, whenever
we can, preach unto men the way of salvation,
setting forth wholesome counsels, and that we
should especially be persevering in prayer and
giving of thanks."

They therefore left the hut for the use of poor
lepers, transferring themselves to Saint Mary of
the Little Portion, very near to which church
they had dwelt for a while in a cottage.

XV. SAINT FRANCIS AT SAINT MARY OF THE ANGELS.

The Blessed Francis, seeing that the Lord wished to multiply the number of the brethren, said to them: "My dearest brethren and little sons, I see that the Lord wishes us to multiply: wherefore to me it seems good and religious that we acquire from the Bishop or from the Canons of San Rufino, or from the Abbot of S. Benedict, some church where the brethren may be able to say their hours, and to have near to it only some small and modest house, made of mud and osier-wattles, where the brethren may be able to rest and work, for this hut that we are in is not fitting or sufficient for the brethren, seeing that the Lord wishes that we add to our number, and especially because we have not here a church in which the brethren may say their hours. And if any brother should die it would not be fitting to bury him here or in a church of secular clergy."

And the words pleased all the brethren.

He went therefore to the Bishop of Assisi and in his presence expressed himself in the same words. To him said the Bishop : " Brother, I have no church which I am able to give to you." And the Canons replied in the same way.

Then he went to the Abbot of S. Benedict of Monte Subasio, and set before him the same request. But the Abbot, moved with pity, having taken counsel with his monks, by the working of the divine grace and will, conceded to the Blessed Francis and his brethren the Church of the Blessed Mary of the Little Portion, it being the smallest and poorest Church which they possessed. And the Abbot said unto the Blessed Francis : " Lo ! brother, we have granted what thou didst ask for. But if the Lord shall multiply your congregation we wish that this place shall be the head of all your houses."

And the speech pleased the Blessed Francis and his brethren, and the Blessed Francis rejoiced very much because of the place granted to the brethren, especially because the name of the Church was that of the Mother of Christ, and because the Church was so small and poor, and because also it was further named "of the Little Portion," in which it was prefigured that it should become the head and mother of the poor Brothers Minor. It was called " the Little Portion," because the courtyard had of old been known as " the Little Portion."

Wherefore the Blessed Francis said: "Therefore hath the Lord willed that no other church
shall be bestowed upon the brethren and that the
first brethren at that time should not build a
quite new church or possess any church but
that, since that therein was fulfilled a certain
prophecy through the coming of the Brothers
Minor." And although it was poor and is now
destroyed, yet for a long time the men of the city
of Assisi and of all that lordship have had great
devotion for that Church, and have greater still
at the present day, and their devotion for it
increaseth daily. Wherefore directly that the
brethren went there to dwell, the Lord multiplied
their number almost daily, and the sweet fragrance
of their fame was marvellously dispersed throughout the whole Vale of Spoleto and through many
parts of the world. Aforetime, however, the
Church was called Saint Mary of the Angels,
because, as it is said, songs of angels were there
often heard.

And although the Abbot and monks had
bestowed the same on the Blessed Francis and
his brethren freely, yet the Blessed Francis as
a good and experienced master, wishing to es-
tablish his house, that is, the religion, upon a firm
rock, that is upon the greatest poverty, did send
every year to the said Abbot and his monks a

basket full of the small fishes that are called
roaches, as a sign denoting great humility and
poverty, as the brethren had no place of their
own, and did not abide in any which was not
within the domain of some others, so that the
brethren had never the power of alienating the
same in any way. But when the brethren took
the little fish to the monks each year, they on
account of the humility of the Blessed Francis,
who did this of his own free prompting, gave
to them a vessel full of oil.

    *   *   *

Although the Blessed Francis knew that the
Kingdom of Heaven had been established in
every part of the earth, and did believe that in
every place divine grace could be given to the
elect of God, yet he had experienced that the
House of the Blessed Mary of the Little Portion
abounded with richer grace and was hovered over
by celestial spirits from on high.

Hence he would often say to the brethren:
"See, O my Sons, that ye never forsake this
House. If ye should be driven out of it on one
side, enter it by another; for this House is sacred
and is the abiding-place of Christ and of His
Virgin Mother. Here when we were few did the
Most High cause us to increase. Here with the
light of His wisdom hath He illumined the souls

of His poor. Here with the fire of His love hath
He kindled our wills. Here he that shall pray
with a devout heart shall obtain what he hath
sought, and he that doth offend shall be the more
severely punished. Wherefore, O my Sons, hold
ye this House with reverence and honour as most
worthy, as the very dwelling-place of God,
especially beloved by the Lord and by His
Mother, and therein with your whole heart, with
the voice of exultation and confession, confess ye
to God the Father and to His Son the Lord Jesus
Christ in the unity of the Holy Spirit."

XVI. SAINT FRANCIS'S IDEAL OF
A PERFECT BROTHER.

The most blessed father being transformed
in a way into the holy brethren, through the
ardour of the love and the fervour of the zeal
which he had for their perfection, often mused
within himself as to the conditions and virtues
wherewith a good Brother Minor should be
adorned. And he was wont to say that he would
be a good Brother Minor who had the life and
conditions of these holy brethren, to wit: the
faith of Brother Bernard, which along with the
love of poverty he had most perfectly; the
simplicity and purity of Brother Leo, who in
truth was of the saintliest purity; the courtesy
of Brother Angelo, who was the first knight
who entered the Order, and was adorned with
every courtesy and gentleness; the graceful bearing and natural instincts with the attractive and
devout eloquence of Brother Masseo; the mind
exalted in contemplation which Brother Giles had
even to the highest perfection; the manly and

continual toilsomeness of holy Rufinus, who without intermission was ever praying, with his mind
whether when he was sleeping or at work upon
anything always with the Lord ; the patience
of Brother Juniper, who attained to a state of
perfect patience by reason of the perfect abandon-
ment of his own will which he ever had before
his eyes, and his transcendent longing to imitate
Christ by the way of the Cross ; the bodily and
spiritual fortitude of Brother John of the Lauds,
who at that time was strong in body above all
men ; the charity of Brother Roger, in whose whole
life and conversation there was the fervour of
charity ; and the solicitude of Brother Lucido,
who was of the greatest solicitude and was unwilling to stay in one place for a month, but
when it pleased him to stay in any place would
straightway withdraw from it, and would say :
" Here have we no place of dwelling, but in
heaven."

XVII.   SAINT FRANCIS AND THE
BROTHERS MINOR.

On a certain occasion the Blessed Francis
said: "The Religion and life of the Brothers Minor
is a certain little flock which the Son of God
in this present hour hath asked of His Heavenly
Father, saying: 'Father, I would that Thou
shouldst make and give to Me a new and humble
people in this present hour, who shall be unlike
in humility and in poverty all others who have
gone before them and shall be content to have
Me alone.' And the Father having hearkened
unto His Son, said: 'My Son, this is done that
Thou hast asked for.'"
Wherefore the Blessed Francis was wont to
say that God had wished and had revealed to
him that they should be called Brothers Minor,
for this reason that the brethren are the people poor
and humble whom the Son of God had asked for
from His Father, as to which people the Son
of God Himself had said in the Gospel : " Fear
not, little flock, for it is your Father's good

pleasure to give you the kingdom." And again :
" Inasmuch as ye have done it unto one of the
least of these My brethren, ye have done it unto
Me." And although the Lord meant this to be
spoken of all spiritual poor men, nevertheless
He especially uttered it of the Religion of the
Brothers Minor which should spring up in His
Church.

Whence, as it was revealed to the Blessed
Francis that it should be called the Order of
the Brothers Minor, so he caused the same to
be written in the First Rule which he took with
him to present to the Lord Pope, Innocent III.,
who approved of it and granted and afterwards
in Consistory announced it to all. In like manner
also the Lord had revealed to him the salutation
which the brethren ought to give utterance to, as
he caused to be written in his testament : " The
Lord hath revealed to me that I ought to say as
salutation : ' May the Lord give thee peace.'"

Wherefore in the early days of the Order
whenever he went with a certain brother who
was one of the first twelve, that brother saluted
men and women by the wayside and those who
were in the fields, saying : " May the Lord give
you peace." And because men had not heard
heretofore such salutation made by any Religious,
they marvelled very much thereat. Yea, some

spoke to them with indignation: "What meaneth such a salutation as this of yours?" So that that brother began thereat to be ashamed, and hence said to the Blessed Francis: "Let me say another salutation." And the Blessed Francis said to him: "Let them talk on, for they do not perceive the things that are of God. But be not ashamed since it will yet be that nobles and princes of this world will show thee and thy brethren great reverence because of this salutation. For it is not a great thing if the Lord should wish to have a new and small people, peculiar and unlike in life and speech all who have gone before, who shall be content to have as their sweetest possession Himself alone."

* * *

Although the Blessed Francis wished his sons to have peace with all men and to present themselves as little children to the whole world, he nevertheless taught by speech and set forth by example that they should be especially humble to the clergy.

For he would say: "We are sent as helpers to the clergy in promoting the salvation of souls, and what in them is found absent should be supplied by ourselves. But let every one receive his reward not according to his authority but according to his labour. Know ye this, brethren, that the gain of souls is most acceptable unto God, and this we are better able to obtain when in peace than when at variance with the clergy. If they, however, hinder the salvation of the people, vengeance is of God, and He will repay them in due time. Wherefore be ye subject to those who are set over you, that as far as dependeth upon yourselves no mischievous zeal spring up amongst you. If ye shall have been sons of peace, ye will gain clergy and people, and this is more acceptable to God than to win the people alone after having scandalised the clergy. Cover (he said) their failings, and supplement their many defects ; then when ye shall have done this, be ye the more humble."

*　　*　　*

When the time of the chapter was drawing nigh, the Blessed Francis said to his companion : " It doth not seem to me that I am a Brother Minor except I am in the state of which I will tell thee. Lo ! the brethren with great devotion invite me to the chapter, and moved by their devotion I go to the chapter with them. But they as they are assembled together entreat me that I set forth to them the Word of God and preach amongst them. And rising up I preach unto them as the Holy Spirit shall have taught me. Now when the preaching is finished

let it be supposed that all shall cry out against
me: 'We will not that thou shalt reign over us,
for thou art not eloquent as would be fitting, and
thou art too simple and foolish, and we are too
ashamed to have so simple and despised a
superior over us, wherefore from this time onward
do not thou presume to call thyself our superior!'
And so they cast me out with revilings and
reproaches. It would seem to me then that I
was not a Brother Minor if I did not rejoice
to the same extent when they should revile me
and cast me out with shame, in their unwilling-
ness that I should be their superior, as much
as when they venerate and honour me, the profit
and advantage to themselves in either case being
held to be equal. For if I rejoice when they exalt
and honour me by reason of their own profit and
devotion, in which nevertheless there may be peril
to my soul, much more ought I to be cheerful and
full of joy as to the benefit and spiritual health of
my soul when they bestow upon me the reviling
in which there is for the soul a sure gain."

*   *   *

Whilst the Blessed Francis was dwelling at
Siena, there came to him a certain doctor of
sacred theology of the Order of Preachers, a
man in every way humble and very spiritual.
When he and the Blessed Francis had conferred

together for some little time on the words of the Lord the master asked of him concerning that word of Ezekiel: "If thou speakest not to warn the wicked from his wicked way, his soul will I require at thine hand." For he said: "Many, good father, do I know who are in mortal sin, to whom I do not announce their wickedness. Will their souls be required at my hand?"

To him the Blessed Francis humbly said that he was a man of simplicity, and that therefore it was more fitting for himself to be taught of him than that he should venture upon a response as to the meaning of Scripture. Then that humble master added: "Brother, although I have heard an exposition of these words from some that are wise, I would nevertheless willingly receive from thee thine interpretation of them." The Blessed Francis therefore said: "If the words are to be interpreted generally, I accept them thus, that the servant of God ought so to burn and shine forth in his life and holiness in himself, that by the light of example and by the language of holy conversation he may reprove all wicked ones. Thus, I say, his splendour and the sweet fragrance of his fame will be an announcement to all of their iniquities."

That doctor, very much edified, as he was departing, said to the companions of the Blessed

AND THE BROTHERS MINOR

Francis: " My brothers, the theology of this man,
upborne by purity and contemplation, is as a flying
eagle, but our learning doth creep on the earth."

*   *   *

The most holy father was unwilling that his
brethren should be eager for knowledge and
books, but wished and preached to them that
they should study to be founded upon holy
humility and to follow pure simplicity, holy
prayer, and our Lady Poverty, on which the first
saintly brethren did build, and this alone he told
them was the safe way for their own salvation
and for the edification of others, since Christ, to
whose imitation we are called, showed us and
taught us by word and by example alike that
this was the only way.

For the blessed father, foreseeing things that
would be, knew by the Holy Spirit and oftentimes
would say to the brethren that " many brothers
led on by the desire perchance of edifying others
will lose their vocation, forsooth holy humility,
pure simplicity, prayer, and devotion, and our
Lady Poverty, and it will happen to them that
they will deem themselves thereby to be more
imbued, that is, filled with devotion and more set
on fire with love and more illumined with the
knowledge of God by reason of their understanding of Scripture. Hence there will be times

131   9—2

when they will remain inwardly cold and empty, and thus they will not be able to return to their earliest vocation because they will have lost the time of living according to their vocation in vain and false study ; and I fear that that which they once seemed to have will be taken from them, because that which was given to them, that is their vocation, to keep to and follow, they will have entirely neglected."

He would say moreover: "There are many brethren who direct all their zeal and all their anxiety towards acquiring knowledge, letting slip their holy vocation by wandering both with mind and body beyond the path of humility and holy prayer. These when they shall have preached to the people and shall have known that thence some are edified or converted to penitence, will be puffed up, and will extol themselves over their work and over another's gain as though it were their own, when however they shall have preached more to their own condemnation and prejudice, and will have worked for themselves nothing in accordance with truth, except as instruments of those through whom the Lord hath verily gathered in the fruit of this kind. For those whom they believe that they have edified and converted to penitence by their knowledge and preaching, the Lord Himself hath edified and converted by the

132

prayers and tears of the holy, poor, humble, and simple brethren, although those holy brethren themselves for the most part do not know it; for such is the will of God that they know it not lest they should thence become proud.

"These brothers are my Knights of the Round Table who hide in deserts and remote places that they may the more devotedly give themselves up to prayer and meditation, deploring their own and others' sins, living with simplicity and having lowly conversation, whose holiness is known unto God and sometimes unknown by their brethren and by others. And when the souls of these shall be presented to the Lord by His angels, then shall the Lord show unto them the fruit and reward of their labours, forsooth the many souls that by their examples, their prayers, and their tears, have been saved, and shall say to them : ' My beloved sons, such and so many are the souls that have been saved by your prayers and tears and examples, and because ye have been faithful over a few things, I will place you over many things. Others indeed have preached and laboured in sermons of their own wisdom, and I through your merits have brought to perfection the fruit of salvation ; wherefore receive ye the reward of their labours and the fruit too of your own merits which is the eternal kingdom which by the violence of your humility and simplicity and of your prayers and tears ye have taken by storm.'

"Thus shall these bearing their sheaves with them—the fruits and merits of the holy humility and simplicity that have become their own,—enter rejoicing and exulting into the joy of the Lord. But they who shall have cared for nothing except to know and to point out unto others the way of salvation, and not at all working out their own salvation, shall stand before the tribunal of Christ, naked and empty, bearing only the sheaves of confusion, shame, and sorrow.

"Then shall the truth of holy humility and simplicity and of holy prayer and poverty which is our vocation be exalted and glorified and magnified, the which truth they who have been puffed up by the wind of knowledge have made light of in their lives and in the vain sermons of their own wisdom, declaring that the truth was falsity, and as being themselves blind have cruelly persecuted those who walked in truth.

"Then shall the error and falsity of their opinions by which they have walked, and which they preached as truth, and by which they have hurled many into the den of blindness, come to an end in sorrow, confusion, and shame, and they themselves with their opinions so densely dark shall be plunged into outer darkness with the spirits of darkness."

Wherefore the Blessed Francis oft would speak upon these words: " Then the barren hath borne many and she who hath had many sons hath become feeble." " The barren is the good Religious who is simple, humble, poor, and despised, who seeming to others to be wretched and forlorn, yet by saintly prayers and virtues continually edifieth others, and bringeth forth with sorrowful sighings."

These words he would very often give utterance to in the presence of the ministers and the other brethren, especially in the chapter general.

XVIII. SAINT FRANCIS AND HIS BRETHREN IN CHAPTER.

In a certain general chapter which Francis the most faithful servant of Christ celebrated at Saint Mary of the Angels, there were assembled five thousand brethren. There were present also Saint Dominic and seven brothers of his Order of Preaching Friars. He was on his way from Bologna to Rome. Having heard that Saint Francis had summoned a chapter to meet on the plain of Saint Mary of the Angels, he desired to be present. There was present moreover the Lord Cardinal Ugolino, who was exceedingly devoted to the Blessed Francis and his brethren. As the court of the Lord Pope was then at Perugia, the said Cardinal was fond of going to Assisi, and on every day he was there he went to see Saint Francis, and sometimes he sang the divine service, and sometimes he preached a sermon to the brethren.

But when he came to visit that holy assemblage, and saw them on the field in bands of sixty and of a hundred and of three hundred,

sitting in divine conference, or kneeling in prayer
and in tears, or in the exercises of charity, and
with such silence that there was there not the
slightest murmuring or rustling heard, he looked
with admiration on so great a multitude, pre-
senting the aspect of a well-ordered line of
encampment, and said: "Truly the camp of God
is here, and this is the army of the knights of
Christ." For there was not heard amongst them
anyone to speak foolish or trifling words, but
wherever they were congregated they were praying, or were in lamentation, or were discoursing
on the salvation of the soul. And they had there
on the field huts roofed over with wattles or
interwoven reeds, arranged in distinct groups according to the various provinces of the brethren.
Wherefore on this account the chapter was called
"the chapter of the wattles," or "the chapter of
the reeds." For beds there was the bare ground,
or a little straw. The pillows were stones or logs
of wood.

By reason of these things the brethren were
thought of with great reverence by those who saw
them or heard their uplifted voices. So great
was the fame of their sanctity that from the Papal
Court then at Perugia, and from other parts of
the Vale of Spoleto many came to see and hear
them. Counts and barons and dukes and knights,

and other gentle folk, and many others, with cardinals also, and bishops and abbots and other clergy, came to see that holy and great and humble congregation. The world had never before seen gathered together such holy men. And chiefly they came to see the very saintly head and father of all those holy men, who had captured from the world such precious booty, and had gathered together such a splendid and devout flock to follow the steps of the venerated adorable shepherd Jesus Christ.

Now all being gathered together, up rose the holy father and venerable leader Francis. In the fervour of the Holy Spirit he set forth the word of life to that happy flock. He spoke in loud and trumpet-like tones, and as though a divine unction were poured upon him. And this theme he expounded: " Great things we have promised, but greater things are promised unto us. Let us observe that which we have promised; let us aspire towards those things that have been promised to us. Fleeting is the pleasure of this world ; long-enduring its punishments. Suffering here is but slight ; glory hereafter infinite." And upon these words he most devoutly preaching, exhorted all to obedience and reverence for the Church as for a saintly mother, and to the sweetness of brotherly love. He bade them pray to God for all people, and exhorted them to acquire patience in adversity, and to live in angelic purity and chastity, and in peace and concord with God and man, and in humility and gentleness with all. He counselled them to think little of worldly things and to have a fervent zeal for evangelic poverty, to be earnest and watchful at times of holy prayer and divine praise, and to cast all care and anxiety of soul and body on the Good Shepherd, the nourisher of our souls and bodies, our Blessed Lord Jesus Christ.

And here he said: "That we may observe these things the better, I command you—all you who as brethren are gathered together here —by the virtue of holy obedience, that no one of you have care or anxiety as to what he shall eat or as to what is needful for the body ; but that ye all devote yourselves earnestly to prayer and praise, casting your every care upon Christ, since He hath special care for you." And when the sermon was ended by Saint Francis, all rendered obedience to his teaching and with cheerful minds began at once to pray.

Now Saint Dominic who was present, wondering at the counsel which Saint Francis had given, and thinking that he was venturing indiscreetly, if indeed as seemed to him in that so great a multitude no one should have a care for the things necessary for the body, and thought that with so large a gathering they would be verging on distress.

But the Lord Jesus Christ, wishing to show that He Himself would take special care of His flock so dear and of His poor ones, inspired to deeds of kindness the dwellers in Perugia, in Spoleto, in Foligno, in Spello, and in Assisi, and in all the country around. They came forth with asses and mules and horses laden with bread and wine, with beans and with cheese, and with all the good things of which they thought the blessed company of the poor would be in need of and would make use of. Besides these they brought napkins and pitchers, great and small, and whatsoever articles there might be a need for ; and he counted himself happy who could render them service the most devotedly and the most attentively, and in all things provide with the utmost zeal for all in that happy multitude things needful for them.

You would indeed have seen there knights and nobles most willingly and devotedly tending that saintly gathering. You would have seen there devout and faithful clergy running about everywhere like men-servants. You would have seen there the flower of the youth of the country around ministering with such great reverence as though they were rendering service not to the poor little brothers, but to the apostles of our Lord Jesus Christ.

When Saint Dominic saw all these things, and recognised that divine providence was really there, humbly reconsidering with himself the before-mentioned utterance as to the indiscreetness of the gathering, which he had made, he, kneeling before the Blessed Francis, acknowledged humbly his error, and said: "Truly God hath taken care of these saintly poor little ones, and I did not know it. Wherefore I now promise to observe holy evangelic poverty, and I in God's name utter a malediction against all brethren of my Order who in the said Order shall presume to have possessions of their own."

For Saint Dominic was very much edified by the faith of Saint Francis and by the obedience and poverty of the so well ordered and so immense a gathering, and by the divine providence and most abundant supply of everything. For as one truly holy and wise, he acknowledged the faithfulness of God in all His words. For as He causes to grow the flowers and lilies of the field, and as He feeds the birds of the air, so does He provide also all things necessary for His devout poor ones.

In this same chapter it was told to Saint Francis that many of the brethren wore leathern corslets next to their bodies, and circlets of iron, by reason of which some were ill, and many were hindered in praying, and some were in a dying state. Wherefore he as a most gentle and loving father, commanded them all by virtue of holy obedience that whosoever wore leathern corslets and iron circlets should take them off in his presence.

There were found quite five hundred leathern corslets and circlets of iron, round the loins and arms. They were in such great quantity that they made one vast heap, and Saint Francis caused them to be left there.

After these things the holy father, teaching and consoling them all, and instructing them how to avoid the evil of the present world, dismissed them all to their various provinces in the world, with the blessing of God and his own benediction, and with the solace of spiritual joy.

To the praise and glory of God.

XIX. SAINT FRANCIS IN PRAYER.

Although for many years he had been afflicted
with infirmities, yet so devout and reverent was he
in praying and at divine service, that during the
time he was at his prayers or reciting the canonical hours, he would never rest against a wall or
against a doorpost, but he would always stand
upright and with bare head, though sometimes on
his knees, and this devotion was the more note-
worthy because he spent the greater part of both
day and night in prayer; yea, even when he was
going about the world on foot he always arrested
his steps when he wished to recite the Hours, and
if he were riding by reason of infirmity he would
always get down to say the Office.

Once it was raining very heavily and he on
account of infirmity and very great necessity was
riding. When he was already altogether wet
through he got down from his horse when he
wished to recite the Hours, and with as great
fervour of devotion and reverence said the Office
while standing in the road and with the rain con-

tinuing to pour upon him, as if he had been in church or in a cell. And he said to his companion: "If the body would fain eat in peace and quietness its food which with the body itself becomes food for worms, with how much quietness and peace, with how great reverence and devotion, ought the soul to receive the food which is God Himself!"

XX. SAINT FRANCIS ANN HIS JOYOUSNESS.

Carried away with the love and compassion of Christ, the Blessed Francis would sometimes do such things as these. For the melody of the spirit within him at its sweetest sparkling out did often give forth sound in the French tongue, and the strain of a divine whispering which his ear had subtly caught would burst forth into a French song of rejoicing.

Sometimes he would pick up from the ground a branch and placing it on his left shoulder would draw another branch used as a bow in his right hand across the same, as though across a viol or other instrument, and making fitting gestures would thus sing in French of the Lord Jesus Christ. But all this fanciful joyous sprightliness would at last end in tears, and this jubilant outburst would dissolve itself in compassion for the sufferings of Christ.

While in these tears he would draw long sighs, and with reiterated laments, forgetful of what he held in his hands, he would be as it were caught up towards heaven.

*   *   *

Now in this the Blessed Francis ever had his highest and chiefest study that away from prayer and the Divine Office he should inwardly and outwardly be continually possessed of spiritual gladness. And this in like manner did he particularly love in the brethren; yea for sadness and despondency, outwardly manifested, did he very often chide them.

For he was wont to say that "if the servant of God would study to have and to keep outwardly and inwardly the spiritual gladness which cometh from purity of heart and is acquired by devoutness in prayer, devils are not able to do him any hurt, for they say: 'When in tribulation and prosperity the servant of God possesseth gladness we are not able to find an entrance whereby we may have access to him, nor can we do him any harm.' But the devils when they are able to quench or in any way to hinder the devotion and gladness which spring out of simple prayer and other excellent works, then they do exult.

"For if the devil is able to have aught of his own in the servant of God, unless he shall be wise and bent upon destroying and cancelling that, by the virtue of holy prayer, contrition, and confession, and satisfaction, in a short time out of a single hair the devil maketh a beam by ever adding thereto. Because, therefore, my brethren,

146

out of cleanness of heart and purity of continual prayer proceedeth this spiritual gladness, to acquiring and preserving these two things special earnest heed must be given, that this gladness which in myself and in you I desire and love with the highest affection to see and feel, ye may be able to have inwardly and outwardly, for the edification of our neighbour and for the confusion of our enemy. For to him and to his limbs it pertaineth to be sad, but to us to rejoice and be glad in the Lord always."

*   *   *

The Blessed Francis was wont to say : "Since I know that the devils envy me for the blessings which God hath bestowed upon me, I do know likewise and see that when they are not able to do me a hurt through myself, they lie in wait and apply themselves to doing me a hurt through my companions. But if through myself and my companions they are not able to do me harm, they fall back with great confusion. Yea, if sometimes I am tempted or full of despondency, when I take note of the gladness of my companion, at once by reason of his gladness am I turned back from that temptation and despondency to inward and outward joy."

The father himself for this reason would severely chide those who presented the outward appearance of sadness. For on a certain occasion he rebuked one of the companions who did appear sad in countenance. And he said to him: "Why dost thou show outwardly grief and sadness because of thine offences? Between thyself and God keep this sadness, and pray to Him that by His mercy He will pardon thee and restore to thy soul the gladness of His salvation of which, since thy sin hath so deserved, it hath been deprived. But in the presence of myself and the others, study always to have gladness, for it becometh not a servant of God to show sadness and a troubled countenance before his brother or any other one."

Not that it should be understood or believed that our father, the lover of all seriousness and seemliness, wished this gladness to be shown by laughter or even by the least idle word, since in this way not spiritual gladness but vanity and frivolity are rather shown forth; yea, in the servant of God he did especially abhor any show of laughter and any idle word, for it was his wish that such a one not only should not laugh but also should not provide the least occasion for laughter in others. Whence in one of his admonitions he hath more clearly set forth of what kind should be the gladness of the servant of God, for he saith: "Blessed is that Religious who hath not joy and gladness except in the most holy words and works of the Lord, and with these doth provoke men unto the love of God in joy and gladness. And woe unto that Religious who delighteth in words that are idle and foolish and with such provoketh men to laughter."

By gladness of countenance, therefore, he would understand the fervour and solicitude and disposition and preparation of mind and body for the doing willingly every good work, since by a fervour and disposition of this kind others at times are more influenced than by the very good deed itself. Yea, if the deed be ever so good, and if it seemeth not to be done willingly and heartily, it more begetteth weariness than provoketh to good.

And therefore he was reluctant to see in the face the sadness that doth too often indicate despondency and indifference of mind and idleness of body as to every good work. But gravity and seriousness in face and in all the members of the body and in the senses he always did especially love in himself and in others, and to this as much as he could by word and example did he lead on others.

For he had experienced that gravity of this kind and modesty of manner were as a wall and a shield very strong against the arrows of the devil, and that the soul without the protection of

149

this wall and shield was as a soldier naked in the midst of foes exceedingly strong and well provided with weapons—foes burning with a ceaseless fury against him and persistently intent upon his death.

* * *

Two years before his death, whilst he was at San Damiano in a certain little cell made of osier wattles, the Blessed Francis on one night prayed thus within himself: "O Lord, be Thou my help; look upon mine infirmities that I may be able to bear them patiently." And he heard the voice of One who said to him: "Brother, be glad and rejoice in thine infirmities and tribulations, and as to aught else be thou as assured as though thou wert already in My kingdom."

And when he arose in the morning he said to his companions: "I am resolved unto the Lord's praise and for our consolation and for the edification of our neighbour to make a new song concerning the creatures of the Lord which daily we make use of, and without which we are not able to live, and as to which mankind doth greatly offend the Creator. Continually are we ungrateful for such great favour, and for so many blessings, by our not praising, as we ought, the Lord, the Creator and Giver of all good things."

And sitting down he began to meditate awhile, and afterwards gave utterance to the canticle

AND HIS JOYOUSNESS

"O Good Lord, Most High, Almighty"
and made music for it and taught his companions
how they should recite it and sing it.

For his spirit was at that time in such great
consolation and sweetness that he wished to send
for Brother Pacifico, who in the world was called
the King of Song, and was the very courtly teacher
of singers, and wished to give him some brothers
that they might go along with him through the
world preaching and singing the praises of the
Lord. For he said that he wished that he who
knew how to preach best among them should
first preach to the people, and that after the
preaching they should all sing with one another
the praises of the Lord as though they were the
minstrels of the Lord.

And when the praises were ended he would
that the preacher should say unto the people:
"We are the minstrels of the Lord, and for these
our songs we wish to be rewarded by you, and,
in this way, that ye enter into true repentance."
And he said: "For what are the servants of God
but as it were minstrels of His that should lift up
the hearts of men and move them to spiritual
gladness!"

And especially did he speak thus of the
Brothers Minor who are given unto the people
of God for their salvation.

XXI. SAINT FRANCIS BLESSING
HIS BRETHREN.

On a time during the very severe illness of the Blessed Francis, his companions, noting his exceeding weakness and his great suffering, thought that he was on the point of dying, and said to him: "Father, what shall we do without thee? Unto whom dost thou leave us orphans? Thou hast ever been a father and a mother unto us, begetting us and giving birth to us in Christ. Thou hast been to us leader and shepherd, master and corrector, teaching and correcting us more by example than by word. Whither therefore shall we go, sheep without a shepherd, orphan sons without a father, men rude and simple without a leader?

"Whither shall we go to seek thee, O glory of poverty, praise of simplicity, honour of our lowliness? Who henceforward will show to us blind men the way of truth? Where will be the mouth that spake unto us and the tongue that counselled us? Where will be the fervent spirit, directing us along the way of the Cross, and strengthening us even towards evangelic perfection? Where wilt thou be, that we may run to thee, the light of our eyes, that we may seek thee, the consoler of our souls? Behold, father, thou art dying! Behold thou dost thus leave us desolate; thus sad and bitterly distressed are we as thou departest from us!

"Behold that day, the day of weeping and bitterness, the day of desolation and sadness draweth nigh! Behold the bitter day which ever since we have been with thee we have feared to see, yea, which we could not even think upon! And of a certainty this is not a marvel, since thy life hath been for us a continual light, and thy words have been torches for ever burning and ever lighting us along the way of the Cross, to evangelic perfection, to the love and the imitation of the most sweet Crucified One.

"And therefore, father, bless us and thy other brethren, thy sons whom thou hast begotten in Christ, and leave unto us some memorial of thy will, that the brethren may have thee ever in remembrance and may be able to say: 'These words did our father leave unto his brothers and sons at his death.'"

Then the most compassionate father, directing

153

his fatherly eyes towards his sons, said to them: "Call unto me Brother Benedict de Pirato." For that brother was a priest holy and discreet, who to the Blessed Francis did celebrate sometimes when he was lying ill, since always when he was able he would wish to have administered to him the holy rite or to listen to its celebration how much soever he might be ill.

And when he had come he said to him: "Write how that I bless all my brethren who are in the Religion, and all those who will come even unto the end of the world. And since by reason of weakness and of the pain of my illness I have not power to speak much, in these three words do I make known to all the brethren present and future, my will and intention. Thus I desire, that in token of my memory and benediction and testament they ever love one another even as I have loved and do love them: that they ever love and observe our Lady Poverty, and ever remain faithful and obedient to the prelates and clergy of the Holy Mother the Church."

For thus our father in the chapters of the brethren was accustomed at the end of the chapter to give his benediction and absolution to all the brethren present and future in the Religion, and also out of the chapter would he many times in the fervour of his charity do the same. Yet he would warn the brethren that they should fear and avoid evil example, and he spoke words of rebuke as to all who by ill example should provoke men to blaspheme the Religion and life of the brethren, causing good and holy poor men to be thereby overcome with shame and severely afflicted.

XXII. SAINT FRANCIS AND
ORLANDO DA CHIUSI.

Saint Francis, in the 1224th year of our
Lord, when he was in his forty-third year, went
from the Valley of Spoleto and betook himself
to Romagna. On his way, when he came to a
certain castle—-the castle of Montefeltro—there
was being celebrated there a great solemnity.
One of the Counts of Montefeltro was to be
knighted. When the holy father had heard this
from one who dwelt near the castle, he said to
Brother Leo who was with him : "Let us go to
this festival, since with the aid of God we may
gather some spiritual fruit." Among the others
who had come to that feast was a certain lord of
Tuscany, who had the name Orlando da Chiusi, of
Casentino, very rich and of noble demeanour,
who by reason of the wonders he had heard of
Saint Francis, had conceived for him great devotion, and desired both to see him and to hear
him preach.

Now Saint Francis, when he had reached the
castle, went into the courtyard, where all the

people of gentle birth were gathered together, and in fervour of spirit mounted the parapet of a wall, and from there preached to the concourse. And for theme he put before them in the vulgar tongue these words :—

"So great the good to which the future me invites
That my sufferings all for me are true delights."

And upon these words the Holy Spirit gave utterance by his tongue, with divine eloquence and with great devoutness. He justified them, forsooth, by the witness of the apostles and by the severe endurances of confessors, and by the many tribulations of holy men and women. All in the courtyard stood listening with minds attentive as though they were hearkening to an angel. Amongst the listeners was the aforesaid Orlando, who rejoiced greatly at the wished-for presence of Saint Francis, and was inwardly touched by his marvellous preaching. He resolved to confer with the holy father concerning his soul's welfare.

Wherefore, at the end of the discourse he said to Saint Francis: "Father, I wish to have converse with thee as to my soul's well-being." But Saint Francis, altogether seasoned with the salt of discretion, said to him: "It pleaseth me much, but go this morning and do honour to thy friends, since they have invited thee to the festival; and after the repast we will speak together as long as thou shalt desire." He assented to this, and after the dinner he took counsel with Saint Francis fully as to things which concerned his own soul's spiritual health. And in the end he said: "Brother Francis, I have a mountain in Tuscany, most fit for devotion and exceedingly solitary, and called Mount La Verna. It is very suitable for those whose desires are for a life of retirement. If that mountain would be acceptable to thee and thy companions, I would freely grant it to thee for my soul's welfare."

Saint Francis was indeed desiring with much longing of heart to find lonely spots, where it would be possible for himself and his companions to devote themselves fittingly to divine contemplation. Having thus heard of the offering, and first speaking words of praise to God who through His faithful ones provides for His little sheep, he then thanked the noble Orlando in these words: "When thou shalt have returned home, I will send two of my companions to thee, and thou shalt show them the mountain and if it shall seem to them a fit retreat for prayer and devotion, I will accept thy charitable offering." For the aforesaid Lord Orlando dwelt in his castle near Mount La Verna.

The aforesaid solemnity having ended, Saint

AND ORLANDO DA CHIUSI

Francis having gone back to Saint Mary of the
Angels and Orlando having returned to his castle
which was called Chiusi and was about a mile
distant from La Verna, Saint Francis sent to
him two of his companions. These sought for
him, but by reason of the district being unknown
to them, it was with great difficulty that they
found Orlando's castle. When however they
found it they were entertained by Orlando kindly
and generously as though they were angels of
God. And by a company of about fifty well-
armed men, to protect them from the wild beasts,
they were led to the mountain of La Verna.
There they looked carefully around, seeking
where they might be able to construct a house
for habitation. They at length found there a
little plateau which they fixed upon in the name
of God as a place suitable to dwell upon. The
men who conducted the brothers finding branches,
they constructed with the same a sort of hut.
And having taken possession of the place they
went for Saint Francis to tell him that the aforesaid place was very secluded and suitable for
divine contemplation.

Saint Francis, hearing this, gave thanks to
God, and taking with him Brother Leo, Brother
Masseo, and Brother Angelo, formerly a knight,
he with them drew nigh to the said mountain.

When he had ascended the mountain with these beloved companions, he rested a little while at the foot of a certain oak.

After a while, rising quite joyful in spirit, he advanced to the said secluded place, where as yet there was nothing but the very poor hut made of the branches of trees.

When Orlando heard that Saint Francis with three companions had climbed up in order to abide on the mountain of La Verna, he felt very great delight, and on the following day he came with many others from his castle to see Saint Francis, and brought with him bread and other food for Saint Francis and his companions. And as he was drawing near to them, he found them praying, and he approached them and saluted them. Then Saint Francis arose, and with the greatest joy and affection received Orlando and his company, and this being done they began to converse together. After they had talked with one another, and Saint Francis had thanked Orlando for the solemn mountain solitudes that he had given them, and for his coming to see them, he begged him that he would have made for him a humble little cell, at the foot of a beautiful beech, which was a stone's throw from the hut of the brothers; for it seemed to him suitable for a devout retreat and fit for prayer. And Orlando at once arranged for this to be done. Then, since evening was drawing nigh and it was time to depart, Saint Francis, before they separated, preached to them for a short while, and ended his discourse by giving them his blessing. Then Orlando, hesitating yet to return, called Saint Francis and his companions apart, and said to them: "My brothers most dear, it is not my intention that in this wild mountain ye shall have to endure bodily needs, such as would render you unable to devote yourselves to things spiritual, and therefore I wish, and this I say to you now for all times, that to my house ye surely send for every one of your needs, and if ye do otherwise, I shall think it very ill of you." And having said this he departed with his company and returned to the castle of Chiusi.

Then Saint Francis made his companions sit on the ground, and taught them as to the manner of life they ought to keep to, both they and whosoever wished to live religiously in seclusion. Amongst other things he imposed on them the observance of holy poverty, saying: "Have not such regard to the charitable offers of my Lord Orlando that ye may in anything offend your lady, Madonna Poverty. Hold for certain that the more we shall shrink from poverty the more will

the world shrink from us, and the more we shall
suffer need. But if we shall embrace and cling
well to holy poverty, the world will follow after
us and nourish us abundantly. God hath called
us into this holy life of religion for the welfare of
the world, and hath made this compact between
us and the world, that we give unto the world a
good example and the world will provide for us
in our need. May we then persevere in holy
poverty, for it is the way of perfection, and the
token and earnest of eternal riches." And after
many beautiful and devout words and instruction
on this matter, he ended thus: "This is the
manner of life which I impose on myself and
on you, and because of this, that I see myself
drawing nigh to death, I purpose to remain in
solitariness and recollectedness with God, and
in His presence to mourn over my sins; and
Brother Leo, when it shall seem good to him,
shall bring me a little bread and water, and on no
occasion allow to come to me anyone from the
outer world; but to such do ye respond for me."
And having said these words he gave them his
blessing and betook himself to the cell beneath
the beech tree, and his companions remained in
the place assigned to them, with the steadfast
resolve to observe the bidding of Saint Francis.

XXIII. SAINT FRANCIS AND THE LADY POVERTY.

Amid the other bright and excelling virtues which prepare a shrine and mansion in man for God, and throw light upon the more excellent and quicker way of advancing towards Him and drawing nigh unto Him, holy Poverty standeth out pre-eminent above all, and by the grace conferred alone upon her putteth into the shade the titles of others, since she herself is the foundation of all virtues, and is the watcher over them too, and amid those virtues having Gospel sanction is Princess by merited rank and fame. It is not therefore for the other virtues to fear the descending of the rain, the onrush of the floods, and the blast of the winds threatening ruin, if they rest upon her as upon an immovable base. And this indeed rightly, since the Son of God, Lord of Virtues and King of Glory, loved her with a special love, went in quest of her and found her, when He Himself was toiling in the work of salvation amongst us on earth. Her in the beginning of His preaching did He set as a light of faith to those entering

163   11—2

the harbour of refuge, and as a stone in the
foundation of His house He first laid her, and the
kingdom of the heavens which the other virtues
receive from Him as a promise to be fulfilled,
she hath had bestowed upon her by Himself
without any delaying. "Blessed," He saith, "are
ye poor in spirit, for yours is the kingdom of the
heavens." Worthily theirs is the kingdom of the
heavens straightway, who possess nothing willingly as their own that is earthly, being specially
intent upon longing after and seeking for eternal
things. Of a necessity he who careth not for
earthly food liveth on food celestial, and he with
happy palate tasteth the sweet food-flakes that
fall from the table of the holy angels, who renouncing all earthly things, counteth them all as
dross, so that he may be worthy to taste how
sweet and soothing the Lord is. This is the true
finding of the kingdom of the heavens and the
sure promise of eternal possession in that same
kingdom, and a certain holy foretaste of future
blessedness.

*   *   *

Therefore the Blessed Francis, as a true fol-
lower and disciple of the Saviour from the very
starting of his conversion, gave himself to the
search for holy Poverty, to finding her, and to
keeping steadfastly to her, with all earnestness,

with all desire, with all untiringness, hesitating as
to nothing adverse, fearing nothing of ill omen,
shirking no labour, turning aside from no bodily
distress, if at length the choice should be given
to him of being able to draw nigh unto her to
whom the Lord had entrusted the keys of the
kingdom of the heavens.

He began perseveringly as a most painstaking
explorer to wander through the streets and squares
of the city, diligently seeking her whom his soul
loved. He questioned those who were standing
there, he asked of those who drew nigh to him,
saying thus: "Hast thou seen her whom my
soul loveth?" But that speech was a mystery to
them, and as though he were one of another land,
not understanding him, they said to him: "O
man, we know not of what thou speakest! Speak
to us in our own language, and we will answer
thee." For there was not in that language for
the sons of Adam voice or sense, to cause them
to be willing to exchange converse with him or
to speak concerning Poverty. They hated her
vehemently, just as they do to-day, and they
could not speak calmly to anyone asking aught
about her. So they replied as to one unknown
to them, and asserted strongly that they knew
nothing of what they were asked.

"I will go," said the Blessed Francis, "to the

great and the wise, and will speak with them, for they know the way of the Lord and the judgment of their God." When he had done so, they answered him still more harshly, saying to him: "What is this new teaching which thou dinnest into our ears? The Poverty whom thou seekest, may she ever be with thee, and with thy children, and with thy seed after thee! But it resteth with us to enjoy delights and to abound in riches, since the time of our life is short, and there is trouble with it, and there is no refuge for man at its end. And we have known nothing better than to be cheerful, and to eat and drink as long as we are alive."

The Blessed Francis, hearing these things, marvelled in his heart, and giving thanks to God, said: "Blessed art Thou, O Lord God, who hast hid these things from the wise and prudent, and hast revealed them unto little ones. For so, Father, hath it seemed pleasing unto Thee. Lord, Father, and Ruler of my life, leave me not a prey to their counsel, and let me not fall under their reproaches, but give me Thy grace to find what I seek, for I am Thy servant and the son of Thine handmaid."

And so wandering forth from the city with a hasty step, the Blessed Francis came to a certain plain, looking over which from afar he saw two old men sitting bowed down with severe sorrow. And when the Blessed Francis came up to them, he said: "Show me, I pray, where the Lady Poverty dwelleth, where doth she take her repasts, where doth she repose at noon, for I languish with love of her."

And they answering said: "Good brother, often have we seen her passing by, since many sought after her. Many at times have associated with her, but often she hath returned alone and naked, adorned with no necklaces, honoured with no escort, clad with no raiment. For she would be weeping most bitterly and would say: 'The sons of my mother have fought against me.' And we would say unto her: 'Have patience, since the righteous love thee.' And now, O brother, climb this mountain great and lofty, where God hath appointed a place for her. For she dwelleth in the holy mountains, because God loveth her more than all the tabernacles of Jacob. Giants have not been able to reach unto her footsteps, and eagles have not flown up to her neck. Poverty is a thing separate, that every man scorneth, because she is not found in the land of those who live softly. Therefore she is hidden from their eyes. She hideth from the birds of the air. God understandeth her path, and her place Himself knoweth. If thou, brother, wishest to draw nigh unto her, strip thee of the garment of thy delight, and lay aside every burden, and the sin that encompasseth thee, because unless thou art naked, thou wilt not be able to climb up unto her who secludeth herself upon so great a height. But because she is full of kindness she is easily seen by those who love her, and found by those who seek her. Attach to thyself faithful companions, that in the ascent of the mountain thou mayst use their courage and be supported by their aid. For woe to one who is alone; if he fall he will have no one to lift him up. If one of several fall, by another shall he be stopped in his fall."

*　　*　　*

Wherefore the Blessed Francis came and chose certain companions, faithful to himself, with whom he came in haste to the mountain. And he said to his brethren: "Come let us ascend to the hill of the Lord, and to the home of the Lady Poverty, that she may teach us her ways, and that we may walk in her paths."

And when from every side they had looked upon the ascent of the mountain, because of its exceeding height and its roughness, some of them spoke one unto another, saying: "Who shall ascend this mountain? and who shall scale its summit?"

AND THE LADY POVERTY

And when the Blessed Francis understood he
said to them: "Straight is the way, my brethren,
and narrow is the gate that leadeth to life, and
few there are who find it. Let us trust in the
Lord, and in the power of His valour, for thus
will be made easy for us everything that is difficult. Lay aside the burdens of your own wills,
and cast from you the load of your sins, and gird
yourselves as men putting forth strength. Forgetful of the things that are behind, reach forth
towards the things that are before as much as
lieth in you. I say unto you that whatsoever
spot your feet shall tread upon shall be yours.
For in truth as a Spirit before our face is Christ
the Lord, who will draw us towards the mountain's summits in the chains of love. Marvellous,
my brethren, is the espousal of Poverty; but
easily shall we be able to have delight in her
embraces, because she, the Lady of the Nations,
hath become as it were a widow, lightly esteemed
and despised, the Queen of all the Virtues. No
one is there in this region who can dare to cry
out, no one who can oppose himself to us, no
one who is able rightfully to forbid us this sacred
converse."

*   *   *

When all these words had been spoken they
all began to walk with one another after Saint

Francis. And when with most easy strides they were hastening towards the summits, lo! the Lady Poverty standing on the very top of that same mountain looked down over the mountain slopes. And seeing these men climbing so strenuously, yea, flying, she marvelled exceedingly, and said: "Who are these who fly like the clouds, and as doves towards their windows? For a long time I have not seen such, and I have not beheld any so untrammelled through having cast away all their burdens. Therefore will I speak to them of the things that have taken a lodgment in my heart, lest they as others should regret having made so lofty an ascent, when they now gaze into the abysses lying around them. I know that they will not be able to seize me with their hands without my consent, but to me there shall be reward in the presence of my Heavenly Father, if I shall give unto them counsel of salvation."

And lo! a voice was heard by her, saying: "Fear not, daughter of Sion, because these are the seed whom the Lord hath blessed, and whom He hath chosen in love unfeigned."

And so, on the throne of her nakedness reclining herself, the Lady Poverty greeted them first with the benediction of sweetness, and said to them: "What may be the cause of your

coming, tell me, my brothers; and wherefore
do ye come so hastingly from the valley of the
wretched to the mountain of brightness? Is it,
perchance, that ye seek me, who, as ye see, am a
poor little one, whirled about by the tempest, far
apart from any consolation?"

*   *   *

But they answered, saying: "To thee we
come, our Lady. We entreat thee to receive us
in peace. We desire to be made servants of the
Lord of Virtues, because He is the King of
Glory. We have heard that thou art the Queen
of Virtues, and in some way we have learnt it by
experience. Wherefore, bending before thy feet,
we beseech thee humbly that thou wilt deign to
be with us, and wilt be unto us the way of drawing nigh unto the King of Glory, even as thou
wast a way for Himself when He deigned to visit
those who were sitting in darkness and in the
shadow of death, dawning from on high. For
we know that thine is the power, thine the kingdom. Thou art appointed by the King of kings,
Queen and Mistress, supreme over all virtues.
Only grant unto us peace, and we shall be saved,
that through thee He may receive us who through
thee hath redeemed us. If thou shalt resolve to
save us we shall henceforth be free. For the
King of kings Himself and the Lord of lords,

Creator of heaven and earth, longed for thy beauty and thy grace. When He was King in His banqueting hall, and rich and glorious in His kingdom, He left His home, He deserted His inheritance. For glory and riches are in His home. And thus from royal seats advancing most honourably, He sought out thee. Great therefore is thy dignity and thy loftiness incomparable, since He, having left all the delights of angels and the boundless excellences of which great was the store in the heights, came to seek thee in the lower parts of the earth, lying in mire, in darkness, and in the shadow of death. Thou wast detestable not a little to all living, and all fled from thee, and as much as they could drove thee from them. And though some could not flee from thee altogether, not the less wast thou hateful to them and by them detested. And after that the Lord, the Ruler, came, taking thee up into Himself, He lifted up thine head amongst the tribes of the people, and adorned thee as a bride with a crown, upraising thee above the loftiness of the clouds. Although of a surety numberless men still hate thee, not knowing thy virtue and thy glory, yet it in no wise harmeth thee, since thou dwellest freely in thy holy mountains in the most sure habitation of the glory of Christ. So hath the Son of the Highest

Father become a lover of thy form, and, clinging
to thee alone in the world, hath proved thee most
blessed among all. For before that He came
from the land of fulness of light to the earth thou
didst prepare a place fit for Him, a throne on
which He might sit, a chamber in which He
might rest, in very truth, a most poor virgin,
from whom He arose and shed His light on this
earth. At His birth, in truth, thou in thy faithfulness didst hasten to meet Him, that in thee,
not in delights, He might find a place acceptable
to Himself. She laid Him, says the Evangelist,
in a manger, because there was no room for Him
in the inn. And thus always thou hast insepar-
ably attended Him, so that in all His life when
He was seen on earth and when He conversed
with men, whilst foxes had dens and birds of the
air their nests, He Himself had not where He
might lay His head. Then when He had opened
His own mouth to teach—He who had formerly
opened the mouths of prophets—amongst the
many things which He spoke, He praised thee
first, He extolled thee first, when He said, 'Blessed
are the poor in spirit, for theirs is the kingdom of
the heavens.' And then also when He would
choose as needful witnesses of His holy preaching and of His glorious mission work for the
salvation of the human race, He chose assuredly

not rich merchants, but poor fishermen, that by such esteem for them He might show that thou shouldst be loved of all. But at length that there might be made known unto all thy goodness, thy magnificence, thy fortitude, how thou surpassest in all virtues, how without thee there can be no virtue, how thy kingdom is not of this world, but of heaven, thou alone didst cleave to the King of Glory then, when all His chosen and beloved ones had timidly forsaken Him. But thou, most faithful spouse, sweetest lover, not for a moment didst thou depart from Him. Yea, thou didst then the more cling unto Him when thou didst the more see Him to be scorned by all. For if with Him thou hadst never been, then would He have been despised by all. Thou wast with Him in the clamours of the Jews, in the insults of the Pharisees, in the reproaches of the chief priests. Thou wast with Him in the buffetings, in the spittings, in the scourgings. He who should have been held in reverence by all was derided by all, and thou alone didst consort with Him. Thou didst not leave Him even in death, the death of the Cross. And on that Cross itself, with body stripped, with arms stretched out, with hands and feet nailed, thou didst suffer with Him, so that naught in Him appeared than thyself more glorious. At last when He departed to heaven, the little seal

174

of the kingdom of the heavens for sealing the elect, He left to thee, that whosoever should aspire to the eternal kingdom should come to thee, should seek thee, should by thee enter therein, since unless signed with the seal can no one enter into the kingdom.

"Therefore, Lady, have compassion on us; sign us with the sign of thy favour. For who is so dull, so unwise, as not to love with the whole heart thee, who art chosen by the Most High, and prepared for eternity? Who will not revere and honour thee, when He, whom all the virtues of the heavens adore, hath adorned thee with such great honour? For who would not willingly adore the marks of thy footsteps, to whom the Lord of Majesty hath so humbly inclined Himself, so companionably joined Himself, with so much love hath clung? We beseech thee, therefore, by Him and because of Him, Lady, despise not our prayers, and our necessities, but from dangers ever deliver us, thou who art glorious and blessed for ever."

*   *   *

To this the Lady Poverty, with a rejoicing heart, and with a face full of gladness, with a sweet voice replied, saying: " I confess to you, my brethren and dearest friends, that from the time ye began to speak, I have been filled with gladness, with overflowing joy, noting your fervour, and knowing already your holy purpose. Your words have been made to me acceptable above gold and much precious stone, and sweeter than honey and the honeycomb. For it is not ye who speak, but the Holy Spirit who speaketh in you, and His unction teacheth you of all things that ye have spoken concerning the King Most High, who alone with His grace hath caught me up into His delight, bearing away my reproach from earth, and amongst the noble ones of the heavens hath glorified me. Therefore I desire, if it wearieth you not to listen, to recount to you the long but not less helpful story of all that hath befallen me, that ye may learn to what extent it behoveth you to walk with and to please God, taking care ye who have desired to put hand to the plough not to look back on the furrow. I am not of brief experience, as many think, but ancient enough, and with a plenitude of days, knowing the order of things, the varieties of creatures, and the variableness of the passing years. I know the swayings of the human heart, partly by the knowledge which time hath brought, partly by subtle insight born within me, partly by the loftiness of the grace given unto me. I myself was for a while in the Paradise of God, where man was naked—yea, I was in man, and with

176

man, in his nakedness, walking amidst all that
spacious Paradise, fearing naught, doubting
naught, conscious of naught that was hostile. I
thought I should be with him ever, since by
the Most High he had been created righteous,
good, and wise, and placed in a region most
pleasant and most beautiful. I was too glad of
heart and festive in mood before him all the time,
because he having nothing of self was all of God.
But alas! undreamt-of evil, utterly unheard of
from the beginning of his being created, entered
stealthily. That unhappy one, who in the midst
of his honour had lost wisdom, and who was
unable to abide in heaven, having entered into
the serpent, by fraud assailed man, so that like
himself he might become a perverter of divine
order. Miserable man gave credence to him as he
counselled evil, acquiesced, consented, and forgat
God his Creator, having first followed the perverter, yea, the transgressor.

"He was first naked, as saith the Scripture of
him, but was not ashamed, because innocence
was complete in him. But when he sinned he
knew himself to be naked, and in his shame
running to the leaves of the fig-trees he made
himself aprons. Seeing therefore my companion
become a transgressor and covered with leaves,
since he had naught else, I removed myself from

him, and, standing afar off, with tearful countenance I began to look upon him. I looked for Him who would preserve me from faintness of courage, and from so great a tempest. And suddenly there was a sound sent forth from heaven, shaking all Paradise, and with it a light of utmost splendour shone forth from heaven. And looking I saw the Lord of Majesty walking in Paradise, when the breath of evening was stirring, brilliant with a glory unutterable and indescribable. And there attended Him multitudes of angels crying with a loud voice, saying : 'Holy, holy, holy, Lord God of Hosts ; all the earth is full of Thy glory !' Thousands of thousands ministered unto Him, and tens of hundreds of thousands attended Him. So that I began, I confess, with fear and exceeding trembling to swoon from utter amazement and horror, and with body shivering, but with heart fluttering, to cry, as from the depths, saying : 'Lord, have mercy ; Lord, have mercy. Enter not into judgment with Thy servant, because in Thy sight shall no one living be justified.'

"And He said unto me : 'Go, hide thyself for a little moment, until mine indignation shall pass away.' And forthwith He called to my companion, saying, 'Adam, where art thou ?' Adam said : 'I heard Thy voice, and was afraid, because

AND THE LADY POVERTY

I was naked, and I hid myself.' Naked indeed
he was, for descending naked from Jerusalem to
Jericho he fell among thieves, who despoiled
him of every excellence with which he had been
born, and leaving him bereft of his likeness to
his Creator. Yet He, the King Most High, but
not the less most merciful, awaited his repentance, giving to him an opportunity of coming
back to Himself. But the wretched one turned
away his heart, breaking forth into words of
malice as he sought out excuses for his sins.
Thus he added to his fault and increased his
punishment, treasuring for himself wrath in the
day of the wrath and of the indignation of the
just justice of God. For he spared not himself
or his seed after him, casting all under the
terrible curse of death. And while all the attend-
ing angels took part in judging him, the Lord
cast him forth from the Paradise of pleasantness,
by a just but not the less a merciful judgment.
And He said to him that he should return to the
earth from which he had been taken. Yet soften-
ing much the sentence of the curse He made for
him coats of skins, betokening in them his
mortality, he having been divested of the garments of innocence.

"Seeing then my companion clothed upon
with the skins of dead creatures, I drew back

from him entirely, inasmuch as he was sent forth
to the multiplying of toils from which he might
become rich. I went on from that time a
wanderer, and was one ever fleeing over the
earth, weeping and lamenting greatly, and from
that time I have not found where my foot might
rest. Abraham, Isaac, and Jacob, and the others
received by promise riches and a land flowing
with milk and honey. In all these things I
sought rest and found it not. For the cherub
with the flaming sword turning every way stood
before the gate of Paradise even until the Most
High should come from the bosom of the Father,
He who sought me as in His sight most worthy.
And He, when He had fulfilled all the things of
which ye have spoken, wished to return to His
Father who had sent Him, and made concerning
myself a testament for His chosen ones, and with
a pronouncement not to be broken, confirmed it,
saying : ' Possess not gold or silver or money.
Carry about with you no purse, no wallet, no
bread, no staff, no sandals, and do not have two
coats. Whosoever will strive with thee in judgment and take away thy coat, let him have thy
cloak also. And whosoever will compel thee to
go with him a mile, go with him also other twain.
Lay not up for yourselves treasures upon earth
where rust and moth corrupt and where thieves

break through and steal. Be not over-anxious, saying, What shall we eat, or what shall we drink, or wherewithal shall we be clothed? Be not over-anxious about to-morrow, for to-morrow shall be anxious as to itself. Sufficient for the day is the evil thereof. Unless anyone renounceth all that he possesseth, he cannot be my disciple'; and other things which are written in the same book."

* * *

At these and many other words the Blessed Francis, with his brethren, fell prone upon the ground, giving thanks to God, and saying: " What thou, our Lady, hast said, is acceptable to us, and as to all that thou hast spoken there cannot be anything taken by us amiss. True is the word which we have heard in our land as to thy words and wisdom. And much greater is thy wisdom than the rumour which we have heard. Happy are thy men and happy are thy servants— they who are ever in thy presence and hearken to thy wisdom. Blessed for evermore be thy God who hath a delight in thee and hath loved thee, and hath appointed thee as Queen that thou shouldest exercise mercy and judgment amongst thy servants. O how good and sweet is thy spirit, checking the wandering and warning the sinning ! Behold, Lady, by the love of the Eternal King with which He hath loved thee, and by that love with which thou lovest Him, we entreat thee that thou wilt not deprive us of our desire, but do with us according to thy mercifulness and gentleness. For great are thy works, and unspeakable. Because of this, unteachable souls stray from thee, and thou advancest alone, on every side unassailable, as a line of encamped forces in battle order, and the unwise are not able to abide with thee. But behold we are thy servants, and for ages upon ages we have sworn and resolved to keep thy righteous judgments."

*   *   *

At these words the heart of the Lady Poverty was moved, and as with her it is ever fitting to have mercy and to spare, not being able to restrain herself further, she ran and embraced them, and offering each one the kiss of peace, she said : " Behold now I come, my brothers and my sons, with you, knowing that I shall, through you, win over many more."

Then the Blessed Francis, not being able to keep silent for joy, began with a loud voice to praise the Omnipotent, who doth not leave them that hope in Him, saying : " Bless the Lord, all ye His chosen ones. Set apart a day of rejoicing, and confess unto Him that He is good and that His mercy endureth for ever."

182

AND THE LADY POVERTY

And descending from the mountain they led the Lady Poverty to the place in which they were abiding ; for it was about the sixth hour.

* * *

And having prepared all things, they pressed her to eat with them. But she said: "Show me first your oratory, your chapter-cloister, your refectory, your kitchen, your dormitory and stabling, your beautiful sedilia, your polished tables, and your great buildings. For I see nothing of these ; but I see you laughing and merry-hearted, over-abounding with joy, filled to the full with consolation as though ye expected all things to be supplied to you according to your wishes." And they answering, said : "Lady and our Queen, we thy servants are wearied from the long journey, and thou in coming with us hast not toiled slightly. Let us, therefore, eat together first, if thou willest, and thus comforted all things shall be fulfilled at thy behest."

"What ye say pleaseth me," she said, "but now bring water that we may wash our hands, and towels wherewith we may dry them."

And they very quickly offered to her the fragment of an earthen bowl, for there was not there a perfect one, full of water. Tilting the broken bowl for the water to flow upon her hands, she looked hither and thither for a towel. And when they could not find one, a brother offered to her the tunic with which he was clad, that with it she might dry her hands. Then she with words of thanks took it, and with her whole heart magnified God who had brought her into companionship with such men.

Then they led her to the place where the table had been got ready. When she had been led thither, she looked and seeing nothing more than three or four crusts of bread of barley and bran placed upon the grass, greatly marvelling, she said within herself: "Whoever saw such things in the generations of the ages past? Blessed art Thou, O Lord God, who hast care for all! Thou art able to do as Thou willest, and Thou hast taught Thy people by such deeds to please Thee."

And so they sat down, side by side, giving thanks to God for all His gifts. And then the Lady Poverty ordered cooked food to be brought on dishes. And lo! there was brought in one dish full of cold water, that all might dip their bread into it. For there was not there a supply of dishes, or a number of cooks.

She begged that at least some fragrant herbs should be brought to her uncooked, but they had not a gardener and knew nothing of a garden, and so they gathered wild herbs in the wood and

placed them before her. She said : "Bring me
a little salt that I may flavour the herbs, as they
are bitter." "Wait a little, Lady," they said,
"until we can go into the city and bring some
for thee, if perchance there be anyone who will
give some to us."

"Bring me a knife," she said, "that I may cut
off what I shall not want, and that I may slice
the bread, which is very hard and dry." They
said to her, "Lady, we have no ironsmith who will
make us swords. But now use thy teeth instead
of a knife, and afterwards we will provide one."

Then she said : "And have you just a little
wine?" And they replied to her and said : "Lady of
ours, we have not wine ; for the life of man hath
for its beginning bread and water, and for thee to
drink wine is not good, for the bride of Christ
ought to shun wine as poison."

After that they were filled, exulting more in
the glory of their scanty supply than they would
have done in the abundance of everything, they
blessed the Lord in whose sight they had found
so great favour, and led her to a place in which
she might repose, for she was wearied. And
so upon the bare ground she cast herself in her
scanty attire. She asked too for a pillow for her
head. But to her at once they brought a stone,
and placed it under her.

SAINT FRANCIS

Yet she slept very quietly and soberly, and when she rose up she hastily sought for the cloister to be shown to her. And they led her to a certain hill and showed her the whole world, as far as it was possible for her to see it, and said : " This is our cloister, Lady ! "

*　　*　　*

She bade them sit down side by side, and then she spoke to them words of life, saying :—"My sons, blessed be ye of the Lord who hath made heaven and earth—blessed be ye who with such great fulness of love have received me into your house, that it hath seemed to me to-day as though I had been with you in the Paradise of God. Therefore am I filled with joy, with over-abounding consolation. And I seek forgiveness because I have been so slow in coming. Truly the Lord is with you, and I knew it not. Behold, what I have longed for, now I see ; what I have desired, now I hold, because I am united to them who on earth represent for me the image of Him to whom I am espoused in the heavens. May the Lord bless your fortitude, and uphold the work of your hands. I pray and entreat you, pressingly, as my dearest sons, that ye persevere in those things which by the teaching of the Holy Spirit ye have begun. Not straying from your perfection as the manner of some is, but avoiding

186

all the snares of darkness, do ye strive ever towards the more perfect things. Very high is your perfection above man, and above virtue, and it illumineth the perfection of men of old with a clearer light. As to possession of the kingdom of the heavens, with you there may be no doubt, there may be no delay, for ye possess already the earnest of your future inheritance, and have received already the pledge of the Spirit, for ye are sealed with the seal of the glory of Christ, corresponding in all things by His grace to that first school of His which, when He came into the world, He assembled together. For what they did in His presence, that same ye altogether in His absence have begun to carry on, and ye fear not to say : 'Lo ! we have left all and have followed Thee.' Nor let the magnitude of the struggle and the immensity of the toil deter you, since ye have a great reward. And looking to the Author and Finisher of all good things, the Lord Jesus Christ, who with the joy set before Him endured the Cross, despising the shame, hold the confession of your hope without yielding. Run to the contest placed before you, in charity. Run with patience, which is especially necessary for you, that by doing the will of God, ye may partake of the promise. For God is powerful to bring to perfection happily the things which, though beyond your own strength, ye have begun by His holy grace, because He is faithful in His promises. Let the spirit which worketh in the children of unfaithfulness find nothing in you; let him find nothing doubtful; let him find nothing faithless; let him not receive from you a cause for exercising his depravity against you. For he is very proud, and his pride and arrogance are more than his strength. He hath great wrath against you, and will turn against you the arms of his whole craftiness, and will strive to pour out for you the poison of his malice, as indeed he who hath already, by warring against others, overpowered them and cast them down, grieveth when he seeth you triumphant over himself.

"Your conversion, dearly beloved, the citizens of heaven celebrate with great joy, and in the presence of the King Eternal they have sung new songs. The angels rejoice in you. The apostles exult, seeing their own life renewed, their doctrines preached, and examples of special sanctity manifested, by you. The confessors dance for joy, knowing that their own victory over the enemy will frequently be commemorated in you. The virgins are glad as they follow the Lamb wheresoever He goeth, and know that their number will be added to by you. The whole celestial court is filled with exultation; for the heavenly host daily celebrate solemnities of new fellow-citizens, and are continually sprinkled with the fragrance of holy prayers ascending from this vale in which ye abide.

"I beseech you, therefore, brethren, by the mercy of God, receive humbly the grace offered to you, worthily using it in all things, ever to the praise, glory, and honour of Him who died for you, Jesus Christ our Lord, who with the Father and the Holy Spirit liveth and reigneth, conquereth and ruleth, God eternally glorious, for ever and ever. Amen."

XXIV. SAINT FRANCIS AND SISTER CLARA.

"The mother of Sister Clara was Hortulana, a fitting name for one who did produce so noble and virtuous a plant in the garden of the Holy Church, which hath taken such increase that her boughs and branches have spread and extended over all the corners of the world, so that the birds of heaven have harboured and built their nests in the boughs thereof, that is a number of religious souls who, soaring up with the wings of virtues, do raise up themselves from terrestrial things, fixing their thoughts on the contemplation of celestial things, sitting on the boughs of this tree to enjoy the shade and shelter thereof, there they remain in heart and affection, with their conversation in heaven.

"Clara, the little plant of Hortulana, fair as the day, and gracious like an angel, began presently to appear and shine like a morning star, or fair Aurora, after the dark night of this world ; for in her tender years and first infancy, she expressed many signs of mature sanctity, whereby

she manifested the goodness of her nature, and
the favour wherewith God had endued her. She
was of nature very tender and delicate, and of
capacity very apt and docile. She learned of her
mother the first grounds of Catholic Religion, the
Holy Ghost by little and little framing this pure
vessel of election till He brought it to fulness of
divine grace and perfection. Her greatest delight
and content was in piety and devotion. In
prayer she seemed to speak to God and His
angels, frequently withdrawing herself from company to pour forth herself in her oratory. There
she laid open her heart and affection to her
Creator, pouring forth rivers of sacred tears from
her eyes.

"She was wholly addicted to the works of
mercy, having a singular affection to the poor
and needy, being not ignorant that he that compassioneth the poor and distressed, compassioneth
Christ Jesus, in their person.

"This celestial dove Clara, hearing the great
fame of the admirable life of Saint Francis, who
then renewed to the world the way of perfection,
with a marvellous example of piety and sanctity,
and considering that many gentle men did follow
him, and that his life was already approved by
our holy Mother the Church, she conceived a
great desire to see and hear him, and to disclose

unto him her generous resolutions. Saint Francis, zealous of the good of souls, and having heard the fame of her virtue, waited the opportunity to meet with her, with intention to frustrate the world of so noble and precious a prey, to present her to our Sovereign Redeemer to serve Him in some notable enterprise as pre-ordained of God.

" She went forth with a good matron, who since her mother's death had governed her in her house (her father being dead too), using such prudent diligence that she found him whom her soul desired, that she might receive from his mouth as from the secretary of the Holy Ghost the divine instructions of her salvation.

" The holy father, having lovingly entertained her, began to preach unto her the contempt of the world, and then he propounded to her chaste ears the honourable and amiable espousals of Jesus Christ, persuading her to conserve the orient pearl of her virginal purity for her heavenly Spouse, who out of that love He bare to us being God became man and would be born of a virgin. His divine words penetrated the soul of this holy damsel. Her heart being set on fire with divine love, she now began very exquisitely to dispose herself to yield to his pious exhortations, which she esteemed to be more than human. The world became irksome unto her, desiring to

192

die unto it. Wherefore beginning already to taste the sweetness of heavenly contemplation, she resolved to embrace a most innocent and holy life. She melted as it were with the love of her heavenly Spouse, after whom she thirsted with a languishing desire.

" The wise and prudent damsel Clara made a holy resolution to set the world at naught, despising and trampling under foot all honours, dignities, marriages, sumptuous apparel, jewels, and all worldly pelf, and to dedicate herself a living temple to Christ Jesus, taking Him for her only Spouse. Having wholly submitted herself to the counsels of the Seraphical Father, she went unto him with great fervour of spirit demanding of him when and in what sort she should make her retire from the world. Whereupon the holy father Saint Francis ordained that on Palm Sunday she should come to the procession with the rest of the people apparelled in most rich and sumptuous manner, and that the night following she should go forth of the city, abandoning all the world, and change the secular pleasures into lamentations of the death and passion of our sacred Redeemer. Upon Palm Sunday this innocent dove came to the procession of the Great Church in the company of her mother and other ladies. What follows is worthy to be recorded,

as being done by the divine ordination, which
was that all the other ladies going, according to
the custom of Italy, to take holy Palm, and Saint
Clara with rare modesty out of a virginal bashful-
ness remaining alone without moving out of her
place, the Bishop descending from the steps of
his seat, put into her hand a branch of Palm, a
true presage and argument of what should befall
to this constant damsel; for our Blessed Saviour
represented by the Bishop would insinuate that
the same night she should ascend to the Palm to
gather the pleasant fruit thereof.

" The noble damsel Clara, the spouse of Jesus
Christ, wholly distrusting in her own forces, greatly
apprehended that her new enterprise would be
assaulted and impugned by her friends and kindred, but calling to mind that for the achieving
of any glorious enterprise there is no means so
secure as to have recourse unto God by holy
prayer, she began with intense fervour and the
profusion of many tears to implore the divine
assistance. Knocking incessantly at the gate of
the divine clemency by fervent prayer, she was
not frustrated of her hope.

" Wherefore the night following Palm Sunday,
the year 1212, the 19th of March, the eighteenth
year of her age, she began to prepare to accom-
plish the command of her spiritual guide and

director Saint Francis, and to make a glorious
flight and honourable retire from the world in
modest company, but it seeming to her impossible
to go forth at the ordinary and chiefest door of
the house, she bethought herself to take the
benefit of a back door which (though it were
dammed and closed up with gross stones and
mighty blocks) she with an admirable courage
and force, rather of a strong man than of a tender
young damsel, herself broke open. Thus then
leaving her father's house, her city, kindred, and
friends, she departed so privately that none had
inkling, or knowledge thereof, and with extra-
ordinary speed she arrived at Saint Mary of
Portiuncula, which is at a distance of two miles
from Assisi, where the Seraphical Father, Saint
Francis, with his Religious, expected her. They
received her with burning wax tapers, singing the
hymn Veni Creator Spiritus. This holy virgin,
who sought her Spouse and Redeemer Christ
Jesus, with lamp not extinct and empty, but filled
with divine love, and incontinently in the self-
same hour and place, having left and abandoned
the impurities of Babylon, gave the world the
ticket of defiance before the altar of the Sovereign
Queen of Angels, where the glorious father, Saint
Francis, cut off her hair, and then clothed her with
a poor habit of the Order ; renouncing the jewels

and gorgeous attire wherewith she was adorned, to be given to the poor. To set forth here the devotion of her mind, and the abundance of internal graces which she received in this investure, and the unspeakable joy of her heart, is a thing altogether impossible.

"This beautiful and chaste damsel, having received the ensigns of holy penance, was conducted by the Seraphical Father to the monastery of Saint Paul, which was of Religious women, attired in black, to remain there till Almighty God had provided another monastery.

"Everyone thought it strange that a damsel of a noble family, beautiful, rich, and in the prime of her years, should abandon all pleasures, pomps, riches, and honours, to embrace and undertake a gross patched habit, vile and contemptible, and most rigid and austere penance. Her nearest kindred deemed it would be to them a great affront if their kinswoman Clara lived in this poor state, which in the light of the blind world seemed miserable. Wherefore coming to the monastery of the Religious women of Saint Paul, they used all the endeavours which enraged folly suggested unto them, to supplant her holy resolution. At last they used threats and attempted to force her to yield and retire from so abject and contemptible a life, protesting it was a

thing unworthy her noble birth, and that such an
absurdity had never been seen in their city; but
with an invincible courage she said unto them:
'Dear friends and kinsmen, when God doth
speak, the world must be silent and give place;
and when God doth call, we must fly to obey,
though to the hazard and peril of a thousand
lives. Christ Jesus hath called me to His service. I will obey Him, and will take Him for
the Spouse of my soul, and never will I settle my
love or affection on any but Him.' To oppose
and withstand their violence, she took such fast
hold of the altar that she drew off the altar cloths,
and uncovering her head she showed how her
hair was cut off, and said that she could not be
separated from the service of her Redeemer for
whose love she had forsaken the world, and them
also, and the more they did vex and torment her
the more would her heart be inflamed in the love
of her God who would minister new forces unto
her to resist and overcome. For many days
together she was assaulted with injuries and
reproaches. But in time they were compelled to
desist and retire with shame and confusion.

"Some few days after she was conducted by
our holy father Saint Francis, in company of two
of his disciples, Brother Philip the Long and
Brother Bernard Quintaval, to the monastery of

the Religious women of Saint Angel of Panso
of the Order of Saint Benedict, near to Assisi.

" Her sister Agnes was converted by her
prayers, and after enduring persecution at the
hands of her kindred, joined her in the monastery,
whither Saint Francis proceeded to admit her with
solemn ceremony.

" By reason that Saint Clara and the Blessed
Agnes, her sister, could not find their hearts content, or enjoy with perfect repose the sweet
embracements of their heavenly Spouse according
to the fervour of their minds amongst the Religious
women of Saint Benedict's Order, they were conducted by their director Saint Francis to the
church of San Damiano, joining to the city of
Assisi, fastening in that place the anchor of their
generous resolutions."

*   *   *

In the early days of his conversion, though
when he had already gathered to him many
brethren, Saint Francis went through a struggle
of great doubt as to whether, forsooth, he should
devote himself to continuous prayer or apply
himself sometimes to preaching. And he desired
especially to know as to this the will and pleasure
of our Lord Jesus Christ. Holy humility however
did not permit him to have confidence in himself
alone, or in the availing power of his own prayers,

and therefore he turned himself humbly, as to a refuge, to others whose prayers would avail in making known as to this matter the divine good pleasure.

Wherefore he called Brother Masseo and said to him: "Beloved, go to Sister Clara, and ask her from me that she, with some one of the more devout and spiritual of her sisters, will, as suppliants, pray to God that He will point out to me that which will be more pleasing to Him, whether that I should sometimes preach, or continuously give myself up to prayer. Go thou also to Brother Silvester who dwells on Mount Subasio, and ask him in like manner." For this Brother Silvester was of such great sanctity that whatsoever he sought for in prayer was immediately granted to him. The Holy Spirit caused him to be singularly worthy for converse with God; therefore Saint Francis regarded him with great devotion and trust. Brother Silvester dwelt on the mountain alone.

Brother Masseo, as he had been bidden by the Saint, placed the aforesaid message first before Saint Clara and afterwards before Brother Silvester. Brother Silvester immediately betook himself to prayer. And when he had prayed he received a divine response. And he went to Brother Masseo, and said: "The Lord saith this, that thou shalt say to Brother Francis, that God hath called him not on account of himself alone, but that he may gather fruit in the world of souls and that through him there may be a great gain of souls." After this Brother Masseo went to Saint Clara that he might know what she had received from the Lord. She replied that both she herself and her sister associate had received from God a response in all things like unto that given to Brother Silvester.

Brother Masseo then returned to Saint Francis. The Saint welcomed him in charity, washing his feet and preparing for him a repast, and after the food had been partaken of, he called him into the wood. With bared head, and hands crossed, on his knees, he asked him, saying: "What doth my Lord Jesus Christ bid me to do?" Brother Masseo replied that both to Brother Silvester and to Sister Clara and her sister one reply of Jesus Christ the Blessed One was made: " That He willeth that thou shalt engage in the work of preaching, inasmuch as God hath not called thee on account of thyself alone, but on account also of the salvation of others."

And then was the hand of the Lord upon Saint Francis. In fervour of spirit he rose up all aflame with virtue from the Most High, and said to Brother Masseo: "Let us therefore be going, in the name of the Lord!"

When Saint Francis had received through Brother Silvester and Sister Clara the divine ordainment to preach, he took for his companions Brother Masseo and Brother Angelo, saintly men. And when he would go as it were with lightning speed, with the impulse of the Spirit, giving no heed to the road or footpath traversed, he came to a castle which is called Cannara. He preached there with such fervour that, on account of that preaching and by reason of the marvellous incident of the twittering swallows, who at his command became silent, from the castle all the men and women flew after him. But Saint Francis said to them: "Do not ye hasten after me, for I will set forth for you what ye ought to do for your salvation." And then it was that he made the resolve to found the Third Order, wherewith to promote the salvation of all everywhere.

* * *

Francis, servant of the Most High God, during the lifetime of the most blessed Clara, very often consoled her with his sacred exhortations. She begged the blessed father Francis that he would grant her this consolation, that, forsooth, they might eat together. But the Blessed Francis always seemed reluctant to consent to this. Whence it happened that the brethren of the holy father, pondering over Saint Clara's desire, said to the Blessed Francis: "Father, it seemeth to us that this unbending resolve of thine is not in accord with divine charity—that it is not so accordant that thou shouldst not hearken, forsooth, to Sister Clara, a virgin so sacred and beloved of God; especially when she herself at thy preaching gave up the luxury of this world. On account of which not only shouldst thou consent that she take food with thee, but also if she were with so much persistence to ask of thee a greater favour, thou oughtest to grant it to her who is of thy spiritual planting."

Saint Francis replied: "It seemeth fitting to you then that I ought to grant her this desire?" They said: "Yes, father; for she is worthy that thou shouldst bestow on her this consolation." Saint Francis answered: "As it thus seemeth to you, it pleaseth me also. But that she may be the more fully consoled I wish that the breaking of bread take place at the sanctuary of Saint Mary of the Angels. For she hath long remained secluded in San Damiano, so that it will be a cause of rejoicing to her to see again the house of Saint Mary where she received the veil and was made a spouse of the Lord Jesus. There, then, we will eat together, in the name of the Lord."

He therefore appointed a day on which the Blessed Clara should come with a sister, his own brethren also accompanying them. And she coming, and having first reverently and humbly saluted the Blessed Virgin Mary, and having wandered in a devotional spirit around the same house, the hour of the repast having arrived, the humble and divine Francis caused the meal to be arranged, as was his wont, on the bare ground. And he himself sat down, and the Blessed Clara and one of the brethren of the holy father, with the sister of Saint Clara, and all his other brethren, were placed around that humble table. But at the first course Saint Francis began to speak of God so sweetly and holily and so sublimely and divinely, that Saint Francis himself and Saint Clara and her sister and all the others who were at that poor little feast, were enwrapt in the over-abundance of the grace of the Highest which descended upon them.

And while they were sitting thus in rapture, and with eyes and hands uplifted towards heaven, to the people of Assisi and Bitonio, and everywhere through the whole neighbourhood, it seemed that the church of Saint Mary of the Angels and the whole house and the wood at that time around the house, were altogether in flames, and that one great fire had seized upon them all.

For which reason, so that they might render help, the men of Assisi ran with haste, believing assuredly that everything was being consumed by fire. But when they reached the house, they saw everything uninjured and untouched. And entering into the precincts they found the Blessed Francis with Saint Clara and all the brethren rapt in God, and all sitting at that humble feast, endued with virtue from on high. And then they perceived of a certainty that it was a divine fire which was kindling within the aforesaid holy men and women, and rendering them all aflame with the full consolation of divine love. Wherefore they went back exceedingly edified and consoled.

But the Blessed Francis and Saint Clara and the rest were refreshed with divine consolation in their souls so abounding, that of the food for the body they touched little or nothing. After this feast of blessedness, Saint Clara, well escorted, retraced her steps to San Damiano. The sisters, when they saw her, rejoiced greatly. For they feared lest Saint Francis might have wished to send her to have the rule over some other convent, as he had already sent her sister Agnes to control as abbess the convent of Monticelli at Florence, and especially as Saint Francis had at one time said to Saint Clara: "Prepare thyself, if there shall be need, to go wherever I shall send thee!" And she, as truly a daughter of obedience, had replied: "I am ready, father, to go whithersoever it shall please thee." And thus it was that the sisters rejoiced much when she returned to them, and henceforth Saint Clara was much comforted in the Lord.

To the praise of Christ. Amen.

       *   *   *

Saint Clara, the most devout disciple and sweetest flower of the Blessed Francis, was of such sanctity that not only the Bishops and Cardinals, but also the Pope, desired with much affection to listen to her and to see her, and often visited her in person. Now on a certain occasion the Pope came to Saint Clara's convent, so that from her who was the sanctuary of the Holy Spirit he might hear celestial and divine discourse. They therefore talked with one another for long concerning the soul's salvation and divine praise. Saint Clara at the same time caused bread to be arranged for the sisters on all the tables, desiring that the loaves should so remain to be blessed by the Vicar of Christ.

When the most holy conference was ended, Saint Clara, kneeling with great reverence, besought the Pope that he would deign to bless the loaves set before him. But the Pope replied:

"Sister Clara, most faithful one, I wish that thou shouldst bless these loaves, and make over them the benediction of Christ, to whom thou hast offered thyself as a complete sacrifice in thine inward soul." She replied: "Most Holy Father, spare me, because in this I should be too much deserving of reproof were I, who am but a humble little woman, to presume in the presence of Christ's Vicar to pronounce such benediction." And the Pope answered: "So that it may not be imputed to thee as a presumption, but especially that thou mayst obtain merit from it, I command thee by the virtue of holy obedience, over these loaves to make the sign of the Cross, and to bless them in the name of our Lord Jesus Christ."

She, as a daughter of obedience, making over the loaves the sign of the Cross, most devoutly blessed them. O marvellous assuredly! that at once on all the loaves appeared a most beautiful sign of the Cross. Of the loaves some were with great devotion eaten and some were kept for the miracle's sake. The Pope especially marvelled at the cross made by the virtuous spouse of Christ, then gave thanks to God, and after that blessed impressively the Blessed Clara.

There were abiding in the said convent Hortulana, the mother of Saint Clara, and Agnes

her sister, and all three were full of the Holy
Spirit, as were also many other holy cloistered
spouses of Christ, to whom Saint Francis sent
many sick persons. By virtue of the Cross, which
with their whole heart they adored, they brought
back to health all as many as were signed with the
sacred symbol.

To the praise and glory of our Lord Jesus
Christ. Amen.

       *   *   *

When the most devout spouse of Christ,
Clara—who indeed was true to her own name,
being of heavenly purity—was seriously ailing in
body, she had to remain within the precincts of
San Damiano, and was not able to go to the
church to keep the canonical hours. When as
the solemnity of the Nativity of our Blessed Lord
Jesus Christ was drawing nigh, when it was the
custom of the sisters to attend matins, and to
devoutly receive afterwards the Holy Communion,
Blessed Clara, while the others went to the solemn
service, remained by herself in her room, in great
weakness, with no small desolation, as she was
not able to be present at such solemn devotions.

But the Lord Jesus, wishing to console His
most faithful spouse, caused her to be present in
spirit in the Church of Saint Francis, both at
matins and at the Holy Communion and also

at every one of the festival solemnities. So that from the chanting of the brethren to the organ-playing at the end she heard everything distinctly. And what is more, she received the Holy Communion, and was fully and abidingly consoled.

But when the sisters, having finished the office in San Damiano, came back to Saint Clara, they said: "O dearest lady Clara, what great consolation we have had on this birth-feast of our Lord and Saviour! Would that thou couldst have been with us!" But she answered: "Thanks I render to my Lord Jesus Christ, my sisters and daughters most beloved, because I too, as ye, have been consoled at all the solemn services of the early morn and at the greater and more important devotions. For by the grace of my Lord Jesus Christ, and with the aid of my blessed father Saint Francis, I have been present in the Church of my father Saint Francis, and with my bodily and with my spiritual ears have heard all the singing and the organ music and above everything have there received Holy Communion. Whereupon at such great favour granted unto me, rejoice with all your hearts, because I both was lying here in weakness and, I know not how, whether in the body or out of the body, I was present, as I have just said, at all the solemnities in the Church of Saint Francis."

AND SISTER CLARA

To the praise of the Lord Jesus Christ.
Amen.

*   *   *

In that week in which the Blessed Francis
departed hence, the lady Clara, the first tender
plant of the poor sisters of San Damiano of
Assisi, the foremost rival of the Blessed Francis
in the Poverty of the Son of God, as she was then
very sick and feared she might die before the
Blessed Francis, wept with sadness of mind and
could not be consoled, because she would not be
able to see before her death her only father, after
God, forsooth, the Blessed Francis, her consoler
and also her first establisher in the grace of the
Lord—the grace conferred upon him by the
glorious Lord Himself before his conversion and
in his holy conversation.

And therefore by a certain brother she made
this known to the Blessed Francis.   Hearing this,
as he loved her and her sisters with a paternal
affection, by reason of their holy conversation,
Saint Francis was moved with pity, chiefly
because after the few years from the time he
began to have the brethren associated with him,
the Divine Lord helping his counsels, she had
been converted to the Lord, from which conversion there was the greatest edification, not
only for the religious life of the brethren,

but also for that of the Universal Church of God.

But the Blessed Francis, thinking that what the lady Clara was longing for, forsooth, to see himself, was not then possible, as both were seriously ill, to console her sent to her by letter his benediction, and absolved her from every failure in obeying his commands and wishes and also the commands and wishes of the Son of God. Especially that she might lay aside every sadness, and be consoled in the Lord, not he, but the Spirit of the Lord through him, spoke these words, delivered to the same brother whom the lady Clara had sent : "Go and bid Sister Clara to put aside every sorrow and sadness, because now she cannot see me. But let her know, that, in truth, before her death, she and her sisters shall see me and shall receive much consolation concerning me."

And so it was that when a little while after, the Blessed Francis passed away in the night, at dawn all the people of the city of Assisi, men and women, with all the clergy, came and bore the holy body from the house where he died, with hymns and praises, each of them carrying branches of trees, and by the will of God thus bore him to San Damiano, that there might be fulfilled the word which the Lord had spoken as to the Saint

for the consolation of His daughters and His
handmaids. And having taken away from the
window the iron lattice through which the handmaids of Christ were accustomed to communicate
and sometimes to hear the word of the Lord, the
brethren took the holy body from the bier and
held it between their arms up to the window for a
long hour, whilst the lady Clara and her sisters
had from it great consolation, although afflicted
with many tears and sorrowings, since after God
he had been their only consolation in this world.

XXV. SAINT FRANCIS AND
SISTER DEATH.

While Saint Francis was lying sick in the palace of the bishopric at Assisi, and while the hand of the Lord did seem to be weighing upon him more heavily than of wont, the people of Assisi fearing lest, if he should die in the nighttime, his brethren might take up his sacred body and carry it away to another city, caused due orders to be made that every night watch should be kept diligently by guards all around the palace wall.

But the most holy father himself, to comfort his spirit lest he should at any moment faint away from the severity of the pain with which he was being continually afflicted, often in the daytime caused the Praises of the Lord to be chanted by his brethren.   This too did he also in the night, for the edification and consolation of the lay-folk who for his sake were keeping watch outside the palace.

Now Brother Elias, considering that the Blessed Francis thus comforted himself in the

SAINT FRANCIS AND SISTER DEATH

Lord and thus rejoiced in the midst of his sickness so great, said to him: "Dearest father, for all this gladness which thou showest for thyself and thy brethren in the midst of thy sickness, I am greatly consoled and edified. But although the men of this city venerate thee as a Saint, nevertheless since they believe firmly that by reason of this thine incurable sickness thou art soon about to die, when they hear the Praises chanted thus by day and by night, they may say to one another: 'How is it that this man who is so nigh unto death showeth such gladness of heart? Surely he ought to be thinking of death.'"

Then said the Blessed Francis: "Dost thou remember when at Foligno thou didst see a vision, and that thou didst tell me that a certain man said to thee that I could not live longer than two years? Before that vision which thou didst see by the grace of God, who suggesteth every good thing to the heart and putteth every good word in the mouth of His faithful ones, I used often to consider my latter end both by day and by night. But from that hour in the which thou didst see the vision I have been more anxious every day to think upon the day of my death." And straightway he said, with great fervour of spirit: "Let me, my brother, rejoice in the Lord, in His praises, and in mine own infirmities, since by the grace of the Holy Spirit I am so united and conjoined with my Lord, that by His mercy I am well able to have joy in Him the Most High.

*   *   *

In those days there visited him in the same palace a certain physician of Arezzo, by name John Good, who was exceedingly familiar with the Blessed Francis. And the Blessed Francis put a question to him, saying: "How seemeth it, to thee, my friend—this sickness of dropsy of mine?" Now he was unwilling to call him by his own name; for he never cared to name anyone who was called Good because of his reverence for the Lord who said: "No one is good but God alone." In the same way he was unwilling to call anyone or to write of anyone in his letters as father or master, by reason of his reverence for the Lord who said: "And call no man father upon earth; nor be ye called masters."

And the physician said to him: "Brother, by the grace of God it will be well with thee." Again did the Blessed Francis speak to him: "Tell me the truth. How seemeth it to thee? Do not fear, for by the grace of God I am not faint-hearted, that I should fear death; for by the help of the grace of the Holy Spirit I am so united with the Lord, that with death and with life I am equally content."

AND SISTER DEATH

Then said to him the physician: "Clearly, father, according to our knowledge of the human body, thy sickness is incurable, and I believe that either at the end of the month of September or on the fourth of the Nones of October thou wilt die."

Then the Blessed Francis, as he lay in bed, spread out his hands towards the Lord and with great gladness of mind and body said : "Welcome, my Sister Death !"

*　　*　　*

After these things, a certain brother said to him: "Father, thy life and conversation hath been and is a light and a mirror not only to the brethren but also to the whole Church, and the same will be thy death ; although to thy brethren and many others thy death may be a matter of sadness and sorrow, nevertheless to thee there shall be consolation and infinite joy, for thou wilt pass over from great toil to greatest rest, from many sorrows and temptations to eternal peace, from the temporal poverty which thou hast loved and to which thou hast perfectly been faithful to true infinite riches, and from this temporal death to perpetual life, where thou shalt see face to face thy Lord God, whom in this world thou hast loved with such great fervour of love and longing desire."

215

Having uttered these words he said to him plainly: "Father, thou knowest of a truth that unless the Lord should send thee from heaven His healing medicine, thy sickness is incurable, and thou hast but a short time to live, even as just now the physicians have already said. But this have I said for the comforting of thy spirit, that ever in the Lord thou mayst rejoice inwardly and outwardly, so that thy brethren and others who visit thee may find thee rejoicing in the Lord always, and so that to those who see this, and to others who hear thereof after thy death, thy death may be a perpetual memorial, even as ever have been and will be thy life and conversation."

Then the Blessed Francis, although he was borne down more than usually by his sickness, nevertheless from these words was seen to derive new gladness of mind, as he heard that Sister Death was so near, and with great fervour of spirit he praised the Lord, saying unto the brother: "If therefore it please the Lord that I should quickly die, call unto me Brother Angelo and Brother Leo that they may sing to me of Sister Death."

When those two brethren had come into his presence, full of sadness and grief, they, with many tears, sang the Canticle of Brother Sun and of the other creatures of the Lord—the Canticle which the Saint had himself made. And then before the last verse of the Canticle he added verses concerning Sister Death:

"Praise to Thee, O my Lord, for Sister Death,
    From whom no one living e'er escapeth.
    Woe be to them that die in mortal sin!
    Blessèd be they who the new life begin,
    At one, O Lord, with Thy most holy will;
    The second death shall not to them do ill."

*   *   *

The most holy father having now both by the Holy Spirit and by the opinion of physicians been certified as nigh unto death, while he was still in the said palace, and feeling himself continually and increasingly being borne down by his sickness, and his bodily strength to fail, caused himself to be carried on his bed to Saint Mary of the Little Portion, so that there he might end the life of the body where he had begun to experience the light and life of the Lord.

But when they who were carrying him had come to the hospice which is on the way, half the distance from Assisi to Saint Mary, he asked them that they should place the bed on the ground, and since by reason of the long and severe weakness of the eyes he was now almost unable to see, he caused them to turn the bed so they might fix his face towards the city of Assisi.

And raising himself a little in the bed, he blessed the same city, saying: "O Lord, as this city of old was, as I believe, the place and habitation of wicked men, so now do I see that on account of Thine abundant mercy in the time acceptable unto Thee Thou hast shown forth singularly in this city the multitude of Thy mercies, and by reason of the goodness within this city alone Thou hast chosen her for Thyself that she may be the place and habitation of those who should know Thee in truth, and should give glory to Thy holy name and show forth unto all Christian people the sweet odour of the good report of holy life, of truest doctrine, and of evangelic perfection. I beseech thee, therefore, Lord Jesus Christ, Father of Mercies, that Thou do not think of our ingratitude, but remember ever the abundant pity which Thou hast extended to her, that always she may be the abode and habitation of those who truly know Thee and glorify Thy name, blessed and most glorious, for ever and ever. Amen."

When he had said these words he was carried to Saint Mary of the Angels, where, having completed forty years of his life and twenty years of perfect penitence, he, in the 1227th year of our

AND SISTER DEATH

Lord, on the fourth Nones of October, departed
to the Lord Jesus Christ, whom with his whole
heart, with his whole mind, with all his strength,
he loved with most fervent desire and with fullest
affection, following Him most perfectly, running
after Him most swiftly, and overtaking Him most
gloriously, who with the Father and the Holy
Spirit liveth and reigneth for ever and ever.
Amen.

XXVI. SAINT FRANCIS AND
THE LADY JACOBA.

When Saint Francis in his last illness, after blessing the city of Assisi, on his way from the bishop's palace, came to Saint Mary of the Angels, he called one of his brethren, and said to him: "Dearest brother, God hath revealed to me, that a few days hence I shall die, and thou knowest that the beloved Lady Jacoba of Settesoli, who is so devoted to our Order, if she were to know of my death, and had not been present at it, would be most inconsolably saddened. Lest therefore she should be sad, make it known to her that if she wisheth to find me alive she should come at once." That brother replied: "Thou hast well said, father, because for the great devotion that she hath for thee, it would be very distressing to her if she were not present at thy death." Then said Saint Francis: "Bring me paper and pen, and write as I shall tell thee: To the Lady Jacoba, servant of the Most High, Brother Francis, the poor little one of Christ, sendeth greeting in the Lord, and the fellowship of the Holy Spirit. Know, dearest lady, that Christ the Blessed One of His grace hath revealed to me that the end of my life is at hand. Wherefore if thou dost wish to find me alive, after thou hast read this letter, hasten to Saint Mary of the Angels. For if thou shalt not have come by such a day, thou wilt not be able to find me living. And bring with thee a shroud of hair-cloth in which to wrap my body, and wax for the burial. I pray thee, likewise, that thou bring to me some of that food which thou wast wont to give me when I was in Rome."

But while these words were being written, it was inwardly revealed to Saint Francis that the Lady Jacoba was then coming to him, and was bringing with her all the aforesaid things. Wherefore he at once said to the one who was writing for him : " Do not write more, for it is not necessary, and put the letter aside." And the brethren wondered why he did not permit the letter to be completed.

And after a little while at the door of the house there was a loud knocking, and Saint Francis sent the porter to open it; and when it was opened, there was the Lady Jacoba, the most noble lady of Rome, with her two sons, who were senators, and with a large escort of other knights. The Lady Jacoba went at once to the infirmary, and was soon at Saint Francis's side. And from her coming Saint Francis had great joy and consolation; and she rejoiced likewise to see him alive and at his being able to speak with her.

Then she made known to him how God had revealed to her at Rome, while she was praying, that his life was drawing to a close, and how he was about to send for her and ask for those things which she said she had brought with her; and she caused them to be brought in to Saint Francis, and gave them to him to eat. And he having eaten and being much comforted thereby, the Lady Jacoba knelt down at the feet of Saint Francis, and took those holy feet marked and adorned with the wounds of Christ, and with such great devotion kissed them and bathed them with her tears, that the brethren who stood around seemed to see the Magdalen herself at the feet of Jesus Christ, and by no means could they withdraw her from him. At length after some time they raised her up and drew her aside and asked her how it was she had come at such a right moment of time, so supplied with all the things that were wanted for Saint Francis both in his life and for his burial. The Lady Jacoba answered that when she was praying in Rome one night, she heard a voice from heaven that said to her: " If thou dost wish to find Brother

Francis still alive, go at once without delay to Assisi, and take with thee the things thou wast accustomed to give him when he was sick at Rome, and carry with thee likewise the things that will be needful for his burial"; "and thus," said she, "have I done."

The Lady Jacoba remained there until such time as Saint Francis passed away from this life, and was buried, and at his burial she rendered him the greatest honour. She with all her escort was present, and took upon herself all the expense of whatsoever was needful. And after some time spent at Rome, during which she cherished the memory of Saint Francis, she again came to Assisi. There, after some time given up to holy penitence and virtuous converse, she died, and, as she herself desired, she was buried in the Church of Saint Francis very devoutly.

XXVII. SAINT FRANCIS'S LOVE
FOR ALL THINGS.

It would take far too long, and it would be impossible, to narrate and even to recollect all that the glorious father Francis did and taught, whilst he lived in the flesh. For who would ever be able to express the supreme affection with which, in all things which are of God, he was animated? Who would suffice to narrate the sweetness which he was wont to enjoy contemplating in all creatures the wisdom, power, and goodness of the Creator? In truth, from this meditation he was very often filled with a marvellous and unspeakable joy, when he beheld the sun, when he looked up at the moon, when he contemplated the stars and the firmament.

O simple piety! O pious simplicity! Towards even little worms he felt a warm affection, since he had read how it was said by one: "I am a worm and no man." And therefore he would pick them up on the roadside and hide them away in a safe place lest they should be trodden on by the feet of passers-by. What shall I say as to other small creatures, when, too, the bees in winter, lest they should perish from the severity of the frost, he would cause to be fed with honey or with wine of the best? The skill of their work and the excellence of their instinct, he would extol as setting forth the glory of God, and with such abundant thanksgiving, that he would very often devote a whole day to singing the praises of them and of other creatures.

For as once the three youths, placed in the furnace of burning fire, invited all the elements of the universe to praise and glorify their Creator, so also this man, full of the Spirit of God, did not cease, in all elements and in all creatures, to glorify, praise, and bless the Creator of all things. What great delight did the beauty of flowers bring to his mind, when he beheld their lovely forms and smelt their sweet fragrance! At once he turned the eye of contemplation to the beauty of that Flower which more brightly in spring-time proceeding from the stem of Jesse has aroused to the recognition of its fragrance innumerable thousands of the departed. And when he came upon an abundance of flowers, he would preach to them and invite them to sing the Lord's praises as if they bloomed with reason.

So also the growing corn and vines, rocks and woods, and all beautiful things of the fields, water outflowing from springs, and plants growing in gardens, and the things, such as earth and fire, air and wind, which are of simplest purity,—to all he would speak, counselling them of divine love and freely exhorting them to devotion. All creatures he saluted with fraternal name, and in a manner surpassing and inexperienced by others he would discern at a glance the hidden things of the hearts of all creatures, as though he were one who had already ascended into the glorious liberty of the sons of God.

Now in heaven, O good Jesus, he with the angels praises Thee as Wonderful,—he who of a surety when dwelling on earth preached of Thee and Thy lovingness to all creatures. For beyond the understanding of men he was affected, when Thy name, O holy Lord, was uttered; and dwelling entirely in joy and full of purest gladness, he surely seemed to be a renewed man and one of another world. Wherefore wherever he found anything written, whether divine or whether human, on the wayside, in the house, or on the pavement, he would most reverently pick it up, and place it in a sacred or honourable place, and with such reverence indeed, lest upon it there might be written the name of God, or aught pertaining to that name. And indeed when one day he was asked by a certain brother for what purpose he had so carefully collected writings of pagans on which there was not the Lord's name, he replied, saying : "My son, because there are letters there, with which the Lord's name may be spelt. The good also, which is there, doth not belong to pagans, or to other men, but to God alone, whose is everything good." And what is not less to be admired, when he had caused to be written some letters of salutation, or for the sake of admonition, he would not suffer any letter, or syllable, though it might often be superfluous, to be struck out, though he would have placed in a missing one.

*   *   *

Among all creatures inferior and insensible Saint Francis had a singular affection for fire, on account of its beauty and usefulness, so that he was never willing to prevent fire from burning anything.

After fire he specially loved water, by which is figured holy penitence and the tribulation by which unclean souls are cleansed, and because the first cleansing of soul is made by the water of baptism. Wherefore whenever he washed his hands, he would choose such a place that the water which fell should not be trod under foot. Also when he walked over stones, he walked with great trembling and reverence, for the love of

Him who is called "the Rock." Whence whenever he repeated that psalm, "Upon a rock thou didst exalt me," he would say with great reverence and devotion: "Under the foot of the rock thou hast exalted me."

To the brother moreover who cut and prepared the logs for the fire he used to say that he should never cut down a whole tree, and that some part of such tree should always remain untouched, for the love of Him who on the wood of the cross did work out our salvation.

In like manner also he would tell the brother who tended the garden that he should not cultivate the whole of the ground for eatable herbs only, but should leave some part of the ground so that it might bring forth green herbs which in their seasons should show forth flowers for the brethren, for the love of Him who is called "the flower of the field and the lily of the valley."

Yea, he would say that brother gardener should always make a beautiful little garden in some part of the grounds, setting and planting there of all sweet-smelling herbs and of all herbs that bring forth beautiful flowers so that they might in their due time invite men who looked upon those herbs and those flowers to the praise of the Lord. For every creature crieth out and exclaimeth: "God hath made me because of thee, O man!"

Wherefore we who were with him used to see him so greatly rejoice inwardly and outwardly as it were in all created things, so that in touching them or looking upon them his spirit would seem to be not on earth but in heaven. And by reason of the many consolations that he then had and aforetime had in things created, a little while before his death he composed certain Praises of the Lord for His created things, to incite the hearts of those who should hear them to the praise of God, and that the Lord Himself in His creatures might by men be praised.

*   *   *

Before all creatures lacking reason he used to love with the greatest affection the sun and fire, for he would say: "In the morning when the sun ariseth everyone ought to praise God who hath created him for our use, since through him our eyes are illumined by day. Again in the evening, when the night cometh, everyone should give praise because of brother fire, since by him our eyes are illumined by night; for we are all as it were blind, and the Lord by these two brothers doth enlighten our eyes; and therefore specially for these and other creatures which daily are useful unto us, we ought to praise their Creator

Himself." And he himself always did so up till the day of his death.

Indeed when he was borne down by great infirmity, he began to sing the Praises of the Lord, which he had made for created things, and afterwards did cause his companions to sing, so that whilst meditating upon the Lord's praises he might become forgetful of the bitterness of his sorrows and infirmities.

And he considered and would say that the sun is more beautiful than other created things and is more than aught else a symbol of our Lord, and he remembered too that in Scripture the Lord Himself is called "the Sun of Righteousness." So, when giving a name to those Praises concerning the creatures of the Lord, which Praises he made when the Lord assured him of His kingdom, he called them "The Song of Brother Sun."

XXVIII. SAINT FRANCIS AND HIS
SISTERS THE BIRDS.

Entirely absorbed in the love of God, the
Blessed Francis, not only in his own soul then
adorned with every perfection of excellence but
also in every creature whatsoever, thoroughly
discerned the goodness of God. For this reason
he was affected with a singular and intimate love
towards the creatures, especially towards those
whom he looked upon as figuring forth something of God or something appertaining to
Religion.

Wherefore before all other birds he loved a
certain little bird, which is called the lark and to
which people commonly give the name "the
cowled lark," and he would say of her: "Sister
Lark hath a hood like a Religious and is a humble
bird, because she goeth blithely along the road to
find for herself a few grains of corn. And if she
findeth them even amongst dung she taketh them
out and eateth them. As she flieth she praiseth
God very sweetly, just as the good Religious who
looking down upon earthly things have their

conversation ever in the heavens and are ever intent upon the praise of God. Like unto the earth are her garments, that is her feathers, and she giveth an example unto the Religious, that they should not possess delicate and coloured garments, but such as are of little worth in price and colour, just as earth is commoner than the other elements."

And since he recognised these resemblances in them he would look upon them gladly. Therefore it pleased the Lord that these most holy little birds should show some sign of affection towards him in the hour of his death. For after Vespers on the evening of the Saturday preceding the night on which he passed away to the Lord, a great multitude of this kind of birds which are called larks came over the roof of the house wherein he was lying, and flying just a little way off did make a wheel like a circle around the roof, and as they sweetly sang did seem to join with him in praising the Lord.

*   *   *

We, who were with the Blessed Francis and have written these things, bring forward this testimony that many times we have heard him say : "If ever I shall speak to the Emperor, I will ask him entreatingly and persuasively that he will for the love of God and of myself make

a special law that no man shall catch or kill
Sister Larks or do any harm to them ; and in like
manner that all the authorities of cities and lords
of castles and towns be required every year on
the day of the Nativity of our Lord to compel
men to throw wheat and other grain along the
roads outside the cities and castles, so that our
Sisters the Larks and other birds as well may
have something to eat on that day of such great
solemnity, and that, through reverence for the
Son of God, whom on such a night the most
blessed Virgin Mary did lay down in a manger
between an ox and an ass, whosoever hath an ox
and an ass shall be required on that night to
provide for them the best of good provender, and
in like manner that on such day all the poor ought
to be abundantly fed with good food by the rich."

For the Blessed Francis had a greater reverence for the Nativity of our Lord than for any
other Christian festival. He would say: "After
that the Lord was born for us, it was necessary for
us to be saved." For that reason he wished that
on that day every Christian should rejoice in the
Lord, and that for the love of Him who gave
Himself for us, all should provide in abundance
not only for the poor, but even also for animals
and birds.

*   *   *

Once, as the Blessed Francis was walking with a certain brother, near to the Lagunes of Venice, he saw a great number of birds perched upon the branches of a tree, and singing aloud. Then said he to his companion: "Our sisters, the birds, praise their Creator; let us therefore go close to them, and sing the canonical hours to the Lord." And when they went quite close to them, the birds did not fly away from where they were perched. But, by reason of the noise they made, the brothers could not hear each other as they sang the hours, and therefore the holy man said to the birds: "Birds, my sisters, stay your singing until we have fulfilled our duty by praising God." The birds at once hushed their singing, and kept silent until the office had been fully recited. Then they received permission from the man of God to resume their song. As soon as he had given them permission, they began again to sing in their wonted manner. This they did on a fig-tree, near to the cell of the man of God.

* * *

When Saint Francis had ascended the mountain of La Verna, with three beloved companions whom he had taken with him, and had rested a little while at the foot of a certain oak, a large number of various birds flew together to the Blessed Francis, with twittering and songs and

clapping of wings. And some perched themselves
above the head, some above the shoulders, some
on the knees, some in the hands, of the holy
father. Seeing this strange marvel the Blessed
Francis said to his companions: "I believe, my
very dear brothers, that it will please our Lord
Jesus Christ if we take our abode on this lonely
mountain, on which our sisters, the little birds,
show so much joy at our coming."

*   *   *

Leaving the people of Cannara much consoled
and disposed to penitence, the Blessed Francis
withdrew from thence, and came to a spot between Cannara and Bevagna. And as he was
passing on, still affected with fervour, he lifted up
his eyes and saw, close by the wayside, trees, in
which were perched so great a multitude of birds
of divers kinds, that in those parts the like had
never before been seen. In the field near to the
tree, a very great number also were to be seen.
Saint Francis, looking upon and marvelling at
this crowd of birds, the Spirit of God coming
upon him, said to his companions: "While you
wait for me here on the road, I will go and preach
to our sisters, the little birds." And he went into
the field to the birds that were resting on the
ground.

And immediately, when he began to preach,

all the birds perched up in the trees flew down towards him, and, together with the others in the field, remained motionless, while nevertheless he himself went amongst them, touching very many with his tunic. Still, not one of them at all moved, as was related by Brother James of Massa, a holy man who received all the before-mentioned details from the mouth of Brother Masseo, who was one of those who then were the companions of the holy father.

To these birds, Saint Francis said: "Ye are much cared for by God, ye birds my sisters, and ye ought to praise Him ever and everywhere, because ye have freedom to fly everywhere, because ye have a twofold and threefold clothing, because ye have plumage painted and adorned, because ye have food prepared without your labour, because song hath been taught you by your Creator, because by the blessing of God ye were preserved in the Ark from perishing, because of the element of air allotted to you. Ye sow not, neither do ye reap, and yet God feedeth you, and He giveth you rivers and springs to drink from, mountains and hills, rocks and spreading trees for refuge, and lofty trees in which to build your nests ; and since to spin or weave ye know not how, He provideth both for yourselves and your offspring the clothing ye need. Wherefore the Creator who conferreth on you so many benefits loveth you much. Therefore take heed, little birds, my sisters, lest ye be ungrateful, and study always to give praise unto God."

At these words of the most saintly father, all those birds began to open their beaks, to spread their wings, and stretch out their necks and reverently to bend their heads to the ground and to show by their songs and motions that the words which Saint Francis had spoken had given them manifold delight. Saint Francis, when he saw this, rejoiced in spirit marvellously, and was struck with wonder at so great a multitude of birds and at the very beautiful variety of them and also with their affection and their harmonious friendliness, and especially in them he praised the Creator of such marvellous creatures, and sweetly invited them to sing their Creator's praise.

When he had finished preaching to them and exhorting them to sing the praises of God, he made over all the birds the sign of the cross, and instantly admonished them to praise God. Then all the birds together flew on high, and in the air together raised a loud and wondrous song; and when they had ended the song they divided themselves into four equal clusters, and flew away in the four directions indicated by the cross made over them by the holy father.

And each cluster as it rose on high with its song so marvellous continued to fly in the same direction; one cluster towards the east, another towards the west, another towards the south, and the fourth towards the north; thus showing that just as they had been preached to by Saint Francis, the future standard-bearer of the Holy Cross, so they divided themselves as to present the apparent form of a cross, and, singing as they kept up the cruciform appearance, they flew away through the four quarters of the world, signifying that the preaching of the Cross renewed by the most holy father would be carried through the whole world by his brethren, who, in the manner of birds possessing nothing of their own on earth, would entrust themselves to the providence of God alone.

XXIX. SAINT FRANCIS AND
BROTHER WOLF.

A certain occurrence marvellous and worthy of constant remembrance happened at the city of Gubbio. For when the most holy father Francis was living there, there was in the outskirts of the same city a terrible wolf of immense size and most fierce when in the fury of hunger. He devoured not only other beasts but also men and women, so that he kept all citizens in such great fright and terror that they all went armed when they went outside the city, as if they were setting forth to direful wars. Nevertheless, even when thus armed they were not able to escape the murderous teeth or the savage fury of the said wolf, when they lucklessly met him, especially if any one did so alone. Wherefore such great terror took possession of all, that scarcely any one dared to go outside the gate of the city.

But God wished to make known the sanctity of the Blessed Francis to the citizens. At a time when the blessed father was there, he, having compassion on the citizens, resolved to go out to

239

meet the wolf. The citizens said to him: "Take care, Brother Francis, not to go beyond the gate, for the wolf who hath already devoured many people will utterly kill thee." Saint Francis, trusting in the Lord Jesus Christ, who rules the spirits of all flesh, unprotected either by shield or helmet, but defending himself with the sign of the holy cross, went out beyond the gate with one of the brethren, placing all his trust in the Lord who enables those believing in Him to walk without any hurt upon the basilisk and viper, and to tread down not only wolves but also lions and dragons.

And thus the most faithful Francis went out fearlessly against the wolf. And behold, in view of many looking on from lofty spots to which they had ascended, the terrible wolf ran with open mouth towards Saint Francis and his companion. The blessed father confronted the wolf with the sign of the cross, and by divine virtue kept back the wolf both from himself and from his companion, and the wolf checked his steps and closed his so savagely open mouth. And at last Saint Francis called to him and said: "Come to me, Brother Wolf, and, in Christ's behalf, I bid thee hurt neither myself nor any other one." Marvellous to relate, it was immediately that Saint Francis made the sign of the cross, that the terrible wolf closed his mouth! And the command being given, he at once prostrated himself at the feet of the saint, with head drooping, already transformed as it were from a wolf into a lamb.

As he was thus prostrate Saint Francis spoke to him: "Brother Wolf, thou hast done much mischief in these parts, and hast perpetrated horrible misdeeds, by mercilessly destroying God's creatures. Not only hast thou destroyed unreasoning beasts, but also, what is more detestable audacity, thou hast killed and devoured men made in the image of God. Wherefore thou deservest to be slain, and put to a dreadful death, as a beast of prey and a man-killer of the worst kind. By reason of thy misdeeds all justly cry out and murmur against thee, and all this city is hostile to thee. But, Brother Wolf, I wish between thyself and these to make peace, so that they shall no longer be hurt by thee, and that they shall forgive thee every past offence, and neither men nor dogs shall pursue thee any more."

And the wolf, by the movements of his body, tail, and ears, and by bowing his head, showed that he would assent in every particular to what the saint proposed. And again Saint Francis spoke to him: "Brother Wolf, as it pleaseth thee to make this peace, I promise thee that I will cause to be given to thee daily sustenance by the people of this city, so long as thou shalt live, so that thou shalt no longer suffer from hunger; for I know that whatsoever wrong thou didst was done through the pangs of hunger. But, my Brother Wolf, inasmuch as I shall obtain for thee such favour, I wish that thou promise me that thou wilt never henceforth injure any creature or man. Dost thou promise me this?"

And the wolf made a manifest sign by bowing his head, that he promised to do the things which were imposed upon him by the saint. And Saint Francis said: "Brother Wolf, I wish that thou pledge thy faith to me that I may be able confidently to believe what thou dost promise." And when Saint Francis held out his hand to receive the pledge of faith, the wolf also raised his front right foot, and softly and gently placed it upon the hand of Saint Francis, thus pledging his faith by the only sign possible to him. Then Saint Francis said: "Brother Wolf, I command thee in the name of the Lord Jesus Christ that thou come now with me, nothing doubting, into the city, to perfect this peace in the name of the Lord."

And the wolf obediently began at once to walk with Saint Francis like a most gentle lamb. Seeing this the people of the city began to be wonderfully astonished; and the tidings at once echoed through the whole city, so that both men and women, great and small, met together in the market-place, for Saint Francis was there with the wolf. A great multitude of people being congregated there, Saint Francis stood up and preached to them a wonderful discourse, saying amongst other things, how on account of sins are such pestilences permitted, and how much more dangerous was the consuming fire of Gehenna which would for eternity devour the lost, than the rage of a wolf, who was only able to kill the body; and how much they should dread being plunged into the infernal abyss, since one small creature could keep in such fear and peril so great a multitude. ''Return ye, therefore, dearest people," he said, "to the Lord, and do fitting penitence, and He will deliver you from the wolf now, and in the future from the abyss of devouring fire."

Having spoken thus, he added: " Hear ye, beloved ; the wolf, who here standeth before you, hath promised me and of his promise hath given a pledge, to be at peace with you and never in any way to hurt you, if however ye promise to give him his daily sustenance. And I, in behalf of Brother Wolf, pledge you my word that he will steadfastly keep the compact of peace."

Then all there gathered together, with a great shout, promised to give food continually to the wolf. And Saint Francis before them all said to the wolf: "And thou, Brother Wolf, wilt thou promise these people to keep the compact, forsooth that thou wilt not hurt any beast or any human being?"

And the wolf, kneeling down, with an inclination of his head, and movements of his body and tail, and with gentle motions of his ears, declared evidently to all that he would keep the promised compact. And Saint Francis said: "Brother Wolf, I wish that as thou didst pledge me thy word concerning this when we were outside the gate, so both here before all this people, that thou pledge thy word that thou wilt keep these promises and that thou wilt not in the least desert me as to the pledge I have made for thee." Then the wolf, raising his right foot, placed it as a pledge of fidelity in the hand of Saint Francis, his surety, in the presence of all standing around.

So great was the wonder amidst the joy of all, both on account of the reverence for the saint, and of the strangeness of the miracle, and especially of the peace established between the wolf and the people, that all shouted to the stars, praising and blessing the Lord Jesus Christ, who had sent them Saint Francis, who by his merits had delivered them from the mouth of the worst of wild beasts, and, setting them free from so horrid a pest, had placed them in peace and quietness.

From that day, therefore, the wolf to the

people, and the people to the wolf, kept the compact arranged by Saint Francis. And the wolf living for two years, and begging his food from door to door, hurting no one, and being himself hurt by no one, was fed as though he lived at court. And the great wonder is this, that never did any dog bark at him.

At length Brother Wolf, growing old, died. At his death the citizens mourned much, because the wolf's peaceful and gentle patience, whenever he passed through the city, recalled to their memory the wondrous virtue and holiness of Saint Francis.

To the praise and glory of the Lord Jesus Christ. Amen.

XXX. SAINT FRANCIS AND THE
SISTERS OF SAINT CLARA.

After that the Blessed Francis had made his "Praises unto the Lord of His creatures," he made also certain holy words with music for the consolation and edification of the Poor Ladies, knowing that they were exceedingly troubled because of his illness. And when he could not visit them personally, he sent those words to them by his companions. For he wished to make known his wishes unto them in those words, as to how forsooth they ought to live and to be of humble conversation and to be of one mind in charity. For he saw that their conversion and holy conversation was not only an exaltation for the Religion of the brethren but also a very great edification for the Universal Church.

Yet knowing that from the very commencement of their conversion they had led a life far too straitened and needy, he had ever been moved with pity and compassion for them. Wherefore in those same words he entreated them that as the Lord had gathered them together into one community for holy charity, holy poverty, and holy obedience, so therein they ought ever to live and at length to die. And specially he counselled them that from the alms which the Lord might bestow on them they should discreetly provide for their own bodily needs with gladness and giving of thanks, and chiefly that those who were in health should be patient in the labours they sustained for their sisters who were ill, and that those who were themselves ill should be patient in their illness.

XXXI. SAINT FRANCIS'S SONG
OF PEACE.

After that the Blessed Francis had composed
the aforesaid Praises of the Creatures which he
had called "The Song of Brother Sun," it happened that between the Bishop and the Mayor of
the city of Assisi a great discord arose, so that
the Bishop excommunicated the Mayor, and the
Mayor caused a proclamation to be made that no
one should sell anything to the Bishop or buy anything from him, or make any contract with him.

The Blessed Francis was ill when he heard of
this, and was moved with pity as to them, especially
because no one tried as a mediator to make peace.
He said to his companions : "Great shame it
is to us as servants of God that the Bishop and
the Mayor thus hate one another, and that no
one cometh forward to make peace between
them." And forthwith he made a verse in the
said Praises on that occasion, and thus recited :

"Praise to Thee, O Lord, for all who pardon bestow
  For Thy love's sake, and valiant are in pain and woe.
  Blessèd are they who mid troubles in peace are found,
  For by Thee, O Most High, they shall with joy be
  crowned."

SAINT FRANCIS'S SONG OF PEACE

Afterwards he called one of his companions and said to him: "Go to the Mayor, and tell him as a message from myself to go to the Bishop's palace with the magnates of the city and with others whom he may be able to take with him."

And on the departure of that brother, he said to two others of his companions: "Go, and in the presence of the Bishop and the Mayor and others who are with them, sing the Song of Brother Sun, and I trust in the Lord that He will straightway humble their hearts, and that they will return to their early love and friendship."

Now when they were all gathered together in the quadrangle of the cloister of the Bishop's palace, those two brethren stood up and one of them said: "The Blessed Francis hath made during his illness 'the Praises of the Lord concerning His Creatures,' to the praise of the Lord Himself and to the edification of his neighbour. Wherefore he entreateth you that you will with great devotion listen to them." And thus they began to recite them and sing them.

Then the Mayor at once stood up, and, with joined hands and arms, listened intently to the verses, as to the Gospel of the Lord, with great devotion, for he had great faith in the Blessed Francis, and great reverence for him.

249

And when the Praises of the Lord were finished, the Mayor said in the presence of them all: "In truth I say unto you that not only the Lord Bishop, whom I wish and ought to have for my lord, but if anyone should have killed my brother or my son, him would I forgive." And thus saying, he cast himself at the feet of the Bishop and said to him: "Behold I am ready in every way to make satisfaction to you, as it shall please you, for the love of our Lord Jesus Christ and of His servant the Blessed Francis."

Then the Bishop responding with welcome raised him with his hands and said to him: "From my office I am expected to be humble, and because I am naturally swift to anger, it behoveth that thou shouldst forgive me." And thus with much kindliness and love they embraced and kissed, each the other.

But the brethren, seeing that what the Blessed Francis had predicted as to their concord was fulfilled to the letter, were amazed and rejoiced. And all the others who were present did ascribe all this, as a very great miracle, to the merits of the Blessed Francis; since the Lord had visited them so quickly, and that they had turned away from such discord and scandal to such concord, without the recalling of a single word.

Now we, who were with the Blessed Francis,

bear testimony that when he said of anyone "thus it is," or "thus it will be," that it always came to pass to the letter; and we have seen so often and so much of what we assert, that it would be long to write of it or narrate it.

XXXII. SAINT FRANCIS—THE INWARD MAN.

O how beautiful, how splendid, how glorious he appeared in innocency of life, in simplicity of words, in purity of heart, in the love of God, in brotherly charity, in passionate obedience, in heartfelt devotion, in angelic aspect! Sweet in manners, placid by nature, affable in speech, appropriate in exhortation, most faithful in another's service, prudent in counsel, capable in affairs, gracious in all things. Serene in mind, gentle in soul, sober in spirit, rapt in contemplation, constant in prayer, and in all things fervent. Constant in purpose, unshakeable in virtue, persevering in grace, and in all things the same. Swift to pardon, slow to wrath, liberal in thought, clear in memory, subtle in dissertation, circumspect in choosing, and simple in all things. Austere towards himself, gentle towards others, discerning towards all.

XXXIII. SAINT FRANCIS—THE
OUTWARD MAN.

A man most eloquent, cheerful in face, in demeanour benign, free from listlessness, without affectation, of moderate stature, verging towards littleness ; head medium-sized and round, face however oblong and prominent, brow smooth and low, eyes neither large nor small, but dark and looking straight out, hair dark, eyebrows straight, nose well formed, delicate, and straight, ears erect but small, temples smooth, tongue peaceful, ardent and eager ; voice strong, sweet, clear, and sonorous, teeth close, uniform, and white, lips not large but thin, beard dark, but not full, neck slender, shoulders straight, arms short, hands small, fingers long, nails lengthy, legs slender, feet small, skin fine, flesh little of it, attire rough, sleep of the briefest, generous - handed. And because he was very humble, he showed every kindness to all men, conforming himself fittingly to the ways of all. More than saintly amongst saints, amongst sinners he was as one of themselves. Aid therefore sinners, lover of sinners, most holy father ; and those whom thou seest lying miserably in the mire of their sinfulness, deign, I pray, most compassionate father, to relieve with thy most glorious supplications.

253

XXXIV. SAINT MARY OF
THE ANGELS.

Before the other Houses of the Order, the Blessed Francis had a singular zeal and a special desire always, as long as he lived, in causing to be maintained every perfection of life and conversation in the Sacred House of Saint Mary of the Angels, as being the head and mother of the whole Order; intending and resolving that that House should be the pattern and example of humility and poverty and of every evangelic perfection to all the Houses.

The House had received its surname "Of the Angels" because it was said that aforetime the songs of angels were there often heard. It had received its third name "Of the Little Portion" because its courtyard had of old been known as "The Little Portion." The Benedictines had called its Church, which was the smallest and poorest they possessed, "The Church of the Blessed Mary of the Little Portion."

*   *   *

SAINT MARY OF THE ANGELS

Of the Privileges which the Lord
granted to the House of Saint
Mary of the Angels.

Holy of Holies this House of Houses,
  Worthily deemed worthy of honours great.
Happy its surname, happier its own name.
  A third name, of gift the sign, ariseth.
Angels here present shed forth light around ;
  Here in nightly watch, hymns their voices sing.
When all in ruins Francis upraised it.
  Of three the Father restored it was one.
This when the sackcloth he put on he chose.
  Here the flesh he forced to obey the mind.
Here with fire of love he kindled our wills.
  Within this Temple the Order had birth.
The Father's guidance men crowd to follow.
  Clara, spouse of God, here her tresses lost,
Cast off pomps of world, so to follow Christ.
  Sisters and brothers thus here first saw light.
Holy Mother bare in them Christ anew.
  Here was made narrow the old world's broad
      way,
And virtue widened in the chosen race,
  Rule outspread, Holy Poverty reborn.

SAINT MARY OF THE ANGELS

Pride cast down 'midst us, the Cross recallèd.
  Where once was Francis troubled and de-
    sponding,
Here was he tranquilled, here his mind renewed,
  Here was shown the truth whereof he doubted;
Yea, here was granted all the Father asked.

XXXV. SAINT FRANCIS IN ECSTASY ON MOUNT LA VERNA.

Saint Francis in his cell on Mount La Verna began more fully to taste and feel the sweetness of divine contemplation. On the festival of the most holy Cross, early in the morning, before dawn, he fell on his knees in prayer in front of the entrance to his cell. Turning his face towards the east he prayed thus: "O my Lord Jesus Christ, I pray thee, grant me two graces, before I die—that I may feel, in my soul and in my body, the pain that Thou, sweet Lord, didst endure in the hour of Thy most bitter passion; and that I may feel in my heart, the exceeding love wherewith Thou, O Son of God, wast inflamed to willingly endure such agony for us sinners."

As he thus continued a long time in prayer, he received the assurance that God would hear him and that it would be granted to him to have the experience he desired. Thus being assured, he began with exceeding great devotion to contemplate the Passion of Christ, and His infinite love; and the fervour of devotion so increased in him that through love and compassion he was completely transformed into the likeness of Jesus.

And as he was thus aflame with contemplative love, he saw descend from heaven a seraph, with six wings of glowing brightness. As the seraph swiftly drew nigh, Saint Francis saw that he bore the image of a man crucified, and that his wings appeared in such wise, that two were spread above his head, two were extended as though for flight, and two were folded over his body. Saint Francis was vividly impressed, and was filled at once with gladness and distress and wonder. He felt glad at the gracious apparition of Christ, who with an expression of lovingness, and with a look of sweet benignity, gazed steadfastly upon him. He felt distress at beholding his Lord on the Cross. He was filled with wonder at a vision so strange and unwonted, knowing well that the weakness of the Passion was little in harmony with the immortality of the seraphic spirit. And while he thus wondered, it was revealed to him by Him who thus became visible to him that this vision had thus presented itself to him by divine ordainment, that he might understand that not by the sufferings of the body but by the burning enthusiasm of the soul, would he be transformed into the express image of Christ Crucified in that marvellous celestial presentation.

258

Then did the whole mount of La Verna appear to be enfolded in flame, which brightened all the hills and valleys around, as though the sun were there resting upon the earth.

After a long and mysterious commune of Saint Francis with his Divine Lord who was thus revealed to him, the marvellous vision vanished away. There was left in the heart of Saint Francis an overpowering fire of divine love, and on his body there was impressed a wondrous semblance and image of the Passion of Christ. Upon his hands and feet there began straightway to appear the marks of the nails, as he had seen them on the body of the Crucified Jesus Christ, in the seraphic apparition ; and on his right side there appeared the resemblance of a still open wound, as though made by a lance.

These sacred wounds gave great joy to his heart, but caused to his body unspeakable pain. He at first tried to conceal the mysterious marks, but could not easily do so from his closest companions.

Just before preparing for his last return to Assisi and Saint Mary of the Angels, Saint Francis called to him Brother Masseo and Brother Angelo, and commended the holy mount of La Verna to their care, and blessed them in the name of Jesus the Crucified One. At their earnest prayer, he suffered them to see, touch, and kiss his hands, adorned with the holy and glorious stigmata ; and then, leaving them consoled and rejoiced, he came down from the holy mount, to which he bade a solemn and touching farewell.

XXXVI. SAINT FRANCIS'S SONG
OF PRAISE.

Most High, Omnipotent, Good Lord! Honour,
   glory, and praise,
And all blessings are Thine alone. To Thee a
   hymn I raise,
Though to utter even Thy name all are unfit
   always.

Praisèd be Thou, my Lord, for all that Thou for
   us hast made.
Praisèd be Thou for Brother Sun, who to dispel
   night's shade
Bringeth us the day and its light, so beautiful,
   so bright,
And whose splendour is symbol of Thy glory to
   our sight.

Praise to Thee, my Lord, for the Moon, whom
   as Sister we greet,
And for the Stars with which Thou dost heaven's
   glory complete.

Praise to Thee, my Lord, for Brother Wind, and
    for Air and Cloud.
Praise to Thee, be sky serene, or tempest rage aloud.
Mid strife and calm, calm and strife, all things
    are sustained in life.

Praise to Thee, my Lord, for Sister Water, humble,
    holy,
Rend'ring service, much prized, to all, e'en to
    the most lowly.

Praise to Thee, my Lord, for Brother Fire, so
    cheerful and bright,
So mighty, so strong, by whom Thou illuminest
    the night.

Praise to Thee, my Lord, for our Sister, dear
    Mother Earth,
Of all the protector, nourisher, and keeper from
    dearth,
Who to grass, and fruits, and flowers of divers
    hues, giveth birth.

Praise to Thee, O my Lord, for all who for Thy
    love's sake
Each other pardon, and of hardship and suffering
    partake.
Blessèd are they who mid tribulation in peace
    are found,
For by Thee, Most High, they shall with eternal
    joy be crowned.

SONG OF PRAISE

Praise to Thee, my Lord, for Sister Death,
  claiming us all.
No man living escapeth her; all must obey her
  call.
Woe to them who die in mortal sin! But they
  who are found
In accord with Thy will most holy, shall be blest
  and crowned ;
The second death shall not them harm, so will
  their joy abound.

O praise ye and bless ye my Lord, and ever
  thankful be,
And serve ye Him with faithful hearts in great
  humility.

This Song of Praise, the greater part of which
was first recited by Saint Francis when he was ill
at San Damiano, is sometimes called "The Songs
of the Creatures," inasmuch as Saint Francis in
its verses gives voice to the praises ever ascending
from all creation to the Creator. Saint Francis
himself calls it "The Song of Brother Sun," and
in its early lines recognises the Sun as a source
of light and beauty, and as transcending in its
splendour all other sacramental symbols of the
Divine Presence in the world.

XXXVII. SAINT FRANCIS AND HIS FRIENDS OF TO-DAY.

The words of this chapter are not those of Saint Francis or of his Umbrian or Italian friends, or of his chroniclers of mediæval times. They are the words of one of his many friends of to-day —the words of one who has often pondered on the theme : What message would a modern Saint Francis deliver to the men and women of the twentieth century ?

The message would be in harmony with the one set forth by word and deed seven centuries ago, but it would not be the same. The note of asceticism would be modified. Even Saint Francis himself confessed before his short earthly life came to an end that he had been unkind towards his bodily frame—that against his Brother Body he had sinned most grievously. The modern Saint Francis would extend a more generous pardon even than that which is placed on record to Brother Elias and to those in sympathy with him, who even in the Saint's time thought that the discipline to which the Order was at first expected to conform was too severe for human nature to bear with. The Saint Francis of our times would see in the Churches of San Francesco at Assisi a monumental appeal for the recognition of this, that the masterful founder of the glorious pile was animated by an overpowering love for the Saint whom he enshrined deep down in the rocky tomb which remained so long hidden and unknown.

This thought as to the reconciliation between the Saint's personal poverty and the splendour of the memorial Churches raised in his honour—a splendour so often contrasted with the Saint's resolve to remain always poor and homeless—a splendour too testifying to the depth and sincerity of the love which was directed towards him in the unseen world—leads on to the statement that the modern Saint Francis would be the apostle of simplicity. It would however be for simplicity in home-life, simplicity in all private personal arrangements, that he would plead. It would be for homely simplicity combined with public splendour; simplicity of family life combined with appealing display in public life; the limitation and ordering of personal needs under a rule of self-denying puritanism, so that thereby the impressive pageantry of civic and ecclesiastical commemorations might be the more brilliantly maintained. It would be a simplicity which would lessen greatly the range of difference existing between the habitations of the poor and the mansions of the rich; a simplicity which would enable the combined wealth of the whole community to be lavished upon all structures within whose walls all could best realise their fellowship with one another, could help one another in the quest of knowledge, could combine with one another to promote the common welfare and impart dignity and beauty to the outer aspects of life.

The modern Saint Francis would advocate simplicity of food—not the simplicity of the Umbrian Saint, touching as it is, as he ate with joy the crusts of charity; but a simplicity which can be associated with thankful enjoyment of all the varied kindly fruits bestowed upon us by mother earth; a simplicity so ordered as to best tend to secure sweetness of health, robustness of frame, and the preservation of the comeliness and lissomness and grace of the human form, so that even extreme old age shall not have associated with it distortions and ravages, but that there shall be a sweet beauty of expression on the faces of the aged harmonising with inward beauty of heart and mind.

The writer of these words was once at Gubbio, the Umbrian hill-side city associated with the

story of Saint Francis and Brother Wolf. At the
very time that he was there the labourers in
the surrounding Umbrian vineyards proclaimed a
strike. One evening, outside the city, he saw that
a placard containing the single word "Sciopero!"
had been affixed to a wall. The next morning
the same ominous placard was to be seen at
frequent intervals on the house walls within the
city, and the pavements too had been stencilled
with the like startling announcement, "Sciopero!"
The local newspapers took part in the agitation
going on, some approving, some lamenting, the
strike; all admitting that distress and trouble
had fallen to the lot of the vineyard labourers.
In and around Gubbio the wolf still raged—the
wolf of extreme poverty, of discontent, of disease.
For in that same neighbourhood too there was
sad evidence that pellagra had made its inroads,
disfiguring the faces, and putting its blight even
upon the minds of Umbrian peasants. There was
need still for a Saint Francis to move through the
streets of Gubbio, to wander amid the Umbrian
vineyards and maize-fields. There was still need
for him to appease the ragings of the wolf, to
speak to the wild creature soothing words, to
allay the discontent, to wave the hand of a transforming blessing over the homes of the poor, to
chase away squalor, to stay the ravages of disease,

267

to bring back smiling contentment and happiness into the lot of toilers. And wherever within or on the outskirts of our modern civilisation the wolf of poverty and squalor and fierce discontent and grim disease is raging, there there is need for a new Saint Francis to come with his soothing, healing, and transforming ministrations.

The modern Saint Francis must in his utterances sound forth a consistent note of joyousness Like the sweet Saint of Umbria he must be ever radiant with cheerfulness. All outward discomfort, the reproaches and taunts even of the envious and malicious, must be borne away on the flood of joy springing forth from the serene depths of a soul full of the peace that passeth all understanding. An outburst of joyousness must sweep away all the annoyances which if met in the spirit which engenders them would but cause them to prolong their mischief and give increased vitality to that which gives them birth. The Saint Francis of to-day must be a preacher of cheerfulness in the midst of poverty, if only the poverty is unallied with squalor and disease, and does not involve deprivation of the ministrations of water and air in all their cleanness and sweetness. For how can men and women be ever submissive to the higher baptism of holy water and of the Divine Spirit, if they are not on the lower plane

268

of life in accordant submission to the cleansing influences of the water of life bubbling from every spring, and to the strengthening and purifying mission of the air of heaven ever moving over the world? There is a poverty from which joyousness has no need to be banished. Such poverty can speak of itself as endowed with the wealth of contentment. It is the poverty which has found itself in sweet alliance with simplicity. "My riches consist in the fewness of my wants" are words that have often found utterance on the lips of lovers of simplicity. They might well have been spoken by the Umbrian Saint. The teaching enshrined in the words may ever be proclaimed by every one upon whom something of the spirit and power of Saint Francis have descended.

The healthy joyousness that the modern friends of Saint Francis should set forth as an essential of the gospel of salvation, will, as it reaches its greatest heights, burst forth into a Benedicite of praise like unto that which once sounded from the hill-sides and valleys of Umbria. The life which throbs in ourselves courses through all creation. We may greet the Sun as our Brother, the Moon as our Sister, and the Stars as our little Sisters too. Air and water, sea and clouds, trees and flowers, rivers and mountains, sea and sky, and birds and beasts of every kind, are all to be saluted as belonging to the great communion of life in which we have our fullest being. They thrill with joy and praise as do we. But their praises are to find highest expression on human lips. The pulsings of our hearts are in harmony with the throbbings of the universal life. We are part of that life, and Saint Francis has taught us to link ourselves to the realms of life encircling us, by the sweet words "Brother" and "Sister." We dwell in the bosom of that life, and that life is ever imprinting its messages on our earnest studious minds, is ever teaching the songs of its loving praise to our hearts so that they may become more and more attuned to the universal harmony. We, like the Umbrian Saint, may win the love of birds and of the wild creatures of the woods, and find our joy in lonely communings beneath the canopy from which our sisters the stars shine out upon us. We with Saint Francis may share the blessing of being caught up into the embrace of that Universal Love, which though its noblest shrine is the throbbing human heart, has its twinkling altar lights scattered throughout the wide expanses, and amid the heights and depths, of creation.

INDEX.

271

INDEX